Great GLYPHS Around the Year

by Honi Bamberger and Patricia Hughes

SCHOLASTIC
PROFESSIONAL BOOKS

New York • Toronto • London • Auckland • Sydney
Mexico City • New Delhi • Hong Kong

Dedication

This book is for all the teachers who have asked us to put into print the ideas for creating glyphs that we have shared with them during workshops. We hope that these ideas will lead you and your students to powerful discoveries about collecting, representing, and analyzing data.

Acknowledgments

We are grateful to Deborah Schecter and Terry Cooper at Scholastic Professional Books for their continued support of the work we do and for helping us share our ideas with teachers. A special thanks to Stephanie Bamberger for her dollar bill glyph, to Stephanie Kramer for her graduation glyph, and to Jodi Moran for her in-line skating glyph.

Cover design by Norma Ortiz
Interior design by Sydney Wright
Interior illustrations by Maxie Chamblis

ISBN 0-590-66263-5

Contents

Introduction

In its new *Principles and Standards for School Mathematics* (released April, 2000), the National Council of Teachers of Mathematics (NCTM) identified Data Analysis, Statistics, and Probability as one of five key content area Standards. This Standard discusses the importance of having students:

☼ pose questions

☼ collect, organize, and represent data to answer questions

☼ interpret data using methods of exploratory data analysis

☼ develop and evaluate inferences, predictions, and arguments that are based on data

This and other Standards are shown in the grid (page 9), correlated to each glyph activity.

For students in Grade 1 through Grade 3, the NCTM objectives and standards can best be met by involving them in meaningful, motivating activities that give them opportunities to collect and represent data in a variety of ways. Creating *glyphs*, pictorial representations of data, provides such a mathematical learning experience.

Great Glyphs Around the Year provides ideas for making glyphs that link with seasonal events and favorite themes for each month of the school year and for some "any time" occasions as well. In this way students can see a familiar context for representing data, such as the Thanksgiving holiday in November or the blooming of spring flowers in May. You can connect various mathematics skills and concepts, and connect mathematics to other school disciplines as well. For example, September's return to school is a perfect time for students to get acquainted by gathering and sharing information about themselves through their school bus glyph activity. In breezy March, with the end of winter approaching, reporting on favorite outdoor activities and creating kites using measurement and geometry skills, are a natural.

What Is a Glyph?

Just as a graph or a Venn diagram conveys information about data that has been collected, a glyph displays collected information in the form of a picture. Taken from the word *hieroglyphics* (picture writing), the details of a glyph describe information about the person who has created it.

Each specific detail of a glyph provides the person viewing it with information. A *legend* allows students to see each feature of the glyph and what it represents.

For example, in our September school bus glyph, the color of the bus represents how the student gets to school each day. If the student rides in a car, the bus is yellow. If the student rides the bus to school every day, the bus is orange. A blue bus indicates that the student rides his or her bike to school each day. And a green bus conveys that the student walks. Other elements, such as the number of the bus and the number of windows on the bus, convey different, specific information.

Once each student has completed his or her own glyph, students can make observations about their own glyphs and the glyphs of their classmates. They can talk about how their glyph is similar or different from others. They can note the attributes of a friend's glyph and write what they know about this person based on the glyph. See page 8 for other ways to extend learning.

Introducing Glyphs to Students

While you may "pick and choose" from the many glyph ideas in this book, teachers often enjoy creating a glyph each month as part of their classroom routine. Primary students enjoy predicting what the next glyph picture might be, based on things that happen at different times of the year.

You will notice that each glyph in this activity book has reproducible blackline masters for you to use. Reproducing the glyph patterns and the legend, and collecting the materials necessary for making the glyph, should be done ahead of time.

When you first introduce glyphs to your students, begin by showing them a completed glyph. Students in primary grades need step-by-step directions when first making glyphs, so it is important to add one feature at a time. For each feature, ask students what the feature means. This will help them focus on what the feature *represents*, not what it *is*.

One way to do this is by reproducing and distributing the legend page of each glyph activity. You can also copy the information on a sheet of chart paper. Be sure to review the legend and the meaning of each symbol or element with students before and after they create their own glyphs. For students who are beginning readers, use the legend yourself and provide directions orally, one step at a time. You might show students how to use a blank sheet of paper to cover the legend steps. Sliding the paper down to reveal one step at a time will help students focus on reading smaller amounts of text.

Using Glyphs With ESL Students

Students who repeatedly hear words in context are more likely to use them and understand their meaning. Beginning with the directions the teacher speaks as each part of the glyph is being described and then constructed, and ending with an analysis of the data each glyph represents, students are exposed to the vocabulary of geometry (shape names, directionality, and position), concepts of measurement (months of the year, time, and money), and number concepts (ordinality, cardinality, even and odd).

While words are consistently used as each glyph is made, the learning potential of glyphs comes in the discussions that follow. As students compare attributes of each glyph, those who are learning the English language hear classmates repeat number words, shape names, and measurement terms, and their own language skills grow.

A Teacher-Student Dialogue

You might follow this routine when introducing glyphs to students for the first time. For each month and each new glyph, modify what you say while still focusing on the questions that are asked and the responses that students make. Questioning keeps the focus on the mathematics of the glyph, rather than the arts and crafts of making it.

Teacher: (*holding up the completed scarecrow glyph so that the whole class can see it*) Children, look at this picture and think of something that you can say about what you see. (*After students have had some time to think, have them whisper what they were thinking to a friend. Then ask them to share with the whole class something they heard or something they were thinking about*).

Child: It looks like a pumpkin with a body on it.

Child: It looks like a scarecrow that would be in a field.

Child: The scarecrow is wearing a hat.

Child: The hat is tipping to the left side.

Child: There are patches on the scarecrow's clothes.

Child: The scarecrow has round eyes.

Teacher: All the attributes you just talked about tell something special about me. This scarecrow is a *glyph*. A glyph tells information about the person who made it. (*Reveal the legend, one item at a time, pointing to each feature on the scarecrow glyph.*) The hat tells you about my first name. The legend says, "Double the number of letters in your first name. How many letters are there?" If there are fewer than 10, the hat tilts to the left; exactly 10, the hat is straight on the head; more than 10, the hat tilts to the right. Look at how the hat is tilted. What does that tell you about the number of letters in my first name, doubled?

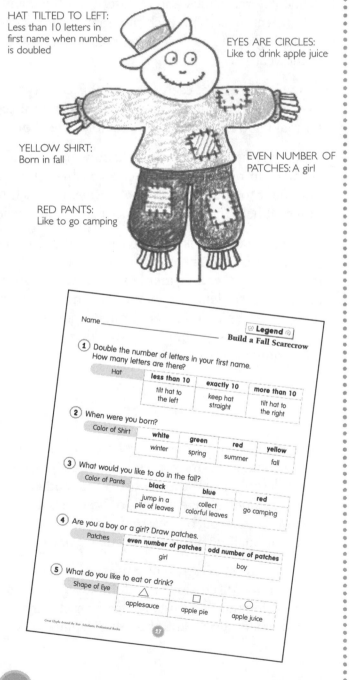

HAT TILTED TO LEFT:
Less than 10 letters in first name when number is doubled

EYES ARE CIRCLES:
Like to drink apple juice

YELLOW SHIRT:
Born in fall

EVEN NUMBER OF PATCHES: A girl

RED PANTS:
Like to go camping

Child: You must have fewer than five letters in your first name. The hat is tipped to the left. Your name doubled has less than ten letters.

Teacher: Now let's look at the color of the scarecrow's shirt. This tells which season I was born in. What are the names of the seasons?

Child: There's spring, summer, fall, and winter.

Teacher: The legend shows that if I was born in the winter the shirt is white; for spring the shirt is green; for summer the shirt is red; and if I was born in the fall, the shirt would be yellow. Look at the scarecrow and figure out which season I was born in, based on the color of the shirt.

Child: You must have been born in the fall because the shirt is yellow.

Teacher: Yes, you're right! Now let's look at the color of the scarecrow's pants, to see what sort of activity I would like to do in the fall. If the pants are black, it means that I would like to jump in a pile of leaves. If the pants are blue, it means that I would like to collect leaves. If the pants are red, it means that I would like to go camping. What would I like to do in the fall?

Child: You would like to go camping.

Teacher: How did you know that?

Child: Your scarecrow has red pants, and the legend shows that red pants means that you like to go camping.

Teacher: How do you know, by looking at my pants, that I don't like to jump in a pile of leaves or collect leaves?

Child: If you liked to collect leaves, the pants would have been colored blue. If you liked to jump in a pile of leaves, your pants would be black. That's what the legend shows.

Teacher: What about the patches on the scarecrow's clothes? What do they tell us about me? Look at the legend and think about the information that you know about me based on the number of patches. (*When the children have had time to think, have them whisper their answer to their partner before asking them to raise their hands to share with the class.*)

Child: There are four patches on the scarecrow's clothes.

Teacher: Yes, and what does that tell about me?

Child: Four is an even number. The legend shows that if you have an even number of patches you are a girl.

Teacher: Okay, now let's review everything you know about me so far, based on the glyph I've made. (*Discuss the legend and have students tell what they have learned.*) Remember that when you are trying to get information from a glyph, the legend reminds you what each part of the glyph represents. Now each of you will make glyphs about yourselves.

Making a Glyph With Students

To successfully make a glyph with students so that it isn't just an arts and crafts activity, but rather a meaningful mathematics experience, reproduce the glyph patterns ahead of time. Many of the glyphs can be pasted or glued onto a sheet of construction paper so that the glyph is constructed on a sturdy backing. Rather than reproducing blackline master patterns for each student, you can also use them as tracing patterns. Simply cut the pieces out, trace them on tagboard, and cut them out for students to use as patterns when they make their own glyphs.

Getting Started

Once students see an example of a completed glyph, and review the legend to learn what each feature reveals, identify each feature, one at a time, and wait for students to color, cut, and paste to create their own glyphs. Then hold up several glyphs, one at a time, and ask the class to explain what each glyph tells about the child who made it. If you do this each time a new feature is added, students begin to learn what each feature represents. This also gives them many opportunities to analyze the data shown on the glyph before they have to do this for the completed glyph. By "making it simpler," all students can say something about the glyph in progress.

Once the Glyph Is Complete—Extending Learning

This is when much of the "real" mathematics takes place. With each glyph in this book you will find suggestions for critical thinking and extension activities that connect the glyph-making to other areas of the curriculum and to more mathematics. We also provide suggestions of literature to connect the activities with reading and language arts.

A good first activity is to have students work in pairs. Pairs can exchange their glyphs and tell what they know about each other based on the glyphs. Older students can write these descriptions and then give them to their partner to read. As they talk and write, students are interpreting and analyzing data.

Another activity to do once all students have completed their glyphs is to brainstorm ways that the glyphs can be sorted. Let students work in small groups, and ask each group to decide on a way they want to sort their glyphs. As each group reports to the class, ask them to show the sorting method, and then discuss the data that is revealed by each way of sorting. Since each glyph has many different attributes, each can be sorted in a variety of ways. After they are sorted the glyphs can be made into a graph and placed on a bulletin board. Write the question on the bulletin board, "How Did We Group Our Glyphs?" and invite students from other classrooms to interpret the data.

With any glyph activity, students can write a story or poem, draw or write about their glyph and their findings in their math journals, or extend the glyph with other symbols to represent additional information.

Feel free to modify elements of the glyphs as needed to make them more appropriate for the students you work with. We have found these activities highly motivating to students. Teachers tell us that students' use of mathematics vocabulary improves as they create glyphs and interpret the data revealed in them. Enjoy!

Correlation of Math Concepts to the Principles and Standards for School Mathematics (NCTM, 2000)

MONTH/GLYPH	CONTENT STANDARDS					PROCESS STANDARDS				
	Number & Operations	Algebra	Geometry	Measurement	Data Analysis, Probability	Problem Solving	Communication	Reasoning & Proof	Connections	Representation
September We're on Our Way to School!	●		●	●	●	●	●	●	●	●
October Build a Fall Scarecrow	●		●	●	●	●	●	●	●	●
November Gobble Up Glyphs!	●	●			●	●	●	●	●	●
December Gingerbread Cookies—Yum!	●		●		●	●	●	●	●	●
January Healthy or Sick?	●	●	●	●	●	●	●	●	●	●
February My Coins Go Jingle Jangle	●			●	●	●	●	●	●	●
March Come Fly With Me!	●	●	●	●	●	●	●	●	●	●
April New Nests for All	●		●	●	●	●	●	●	●	●
May Flowers Spring Up Everywhere!	●	●		●	●	●	●	●	●	●
June Graduation Day				●		●	●	●	●	●
Summer Make a Summertime Splash!	●		●		●	●	●	●	●	●
Any Time What Time Is It?	●			●	●	●	●	●	●	●
Any Time A Valuable Glyph	●			●	●	●	●	●	●	●
Any Time Brush Up on Glyphs!	●			●	●	●	●	●	●	●
Any Time Roll 'Em!				●	●	●	●	●	●	●

We're on Our Way to School!

ORANGE BUS:
Get to school by bus

FOUR WINDOWS:
One sister goes to this school

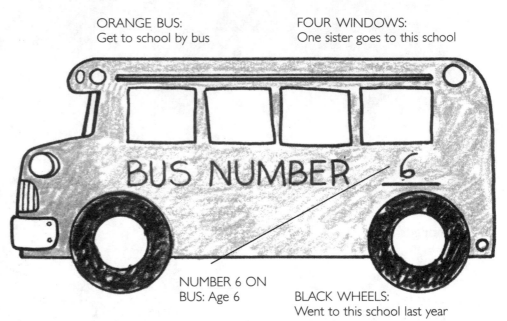

NUMBER 6 ON
BUS: Age 6

BLACK WHEELS:
Went to this school last year

Creating the Glyph

Distribute copies of the school bus glyph patterns and the legend to students. Review the legend, one characteristic at a time, as you display a glyph you have completed. Then distribute the other materials, and invite students to use the legend to create their own personal school bus glyph.

Critical Thinking

Display four completed school bus glyphs. The four should have the following features:

☀ A yellow bus with the number 6, black wheels, and one window.

☀ An orange bus with the number 6, black wheels, and two windows.

☀ An orange bus with the number 6, brown wheels, and two windows.

☀ A green bus with the number 6, brown wheels, and four windows.

Use the following logic problem, revealing one clue at a time. After each clue is revealed, ask students which of the school buses needs to be eliminated, based on the clue and the information from the glyph.

Which School Bus Is Mine?

I am six years old.

I ride on a bus to get to school each day.

I have at least one brother or at least one
sister who goes to this school.

I did not go to this school last year.

(Answer: the third school bus displayed)

School Bus by Donald Crews. William Morrow and Company, 1984. Students follow the path of a school bus on its daily route. Simple text and supporting illustrations help young readers interpret the text.

Explore More

☼ **Home/School** Use this glyph activity at Back-to-School Night. Reproduce a pattern and legend for each family, explain the activity, and ask family members to symbolize information about their child, using the glyph.

☼ **Music/Math** Teach students the words and tune to "The Wheels on the Bus" song. Write the first stanza on chart paper and have them read along with you.

The wheels on the bus go round and round,
Round and round, round and round.
The wheels on the bus go round and round,
All through the town.

The driver on the bus says, "Move on back..."
The children on the bus say, "Yak, yak, yak..."
The mommies on the bus say, "Shh, shh, shh..."

Ask students to identify and count the "objects" (wheels, people, etc.) on the bus in the complete song.

Name _____

1 How do you get to school?

Color of Bus	yellow	orange	blue	green
	in a car	by bus	by bike	walk

2 Did you go to this school last year?

Color of Wheels	black	brown
	yes	no

3 How old are you?

Number on Bus	6	7	8	9
	six years old	seven years old	eight years old	nine years old

4 Who else in your family goes to this school?

Number of Windows	4	3	2	1
	one sister	one brother	more than one brother or sister	only me

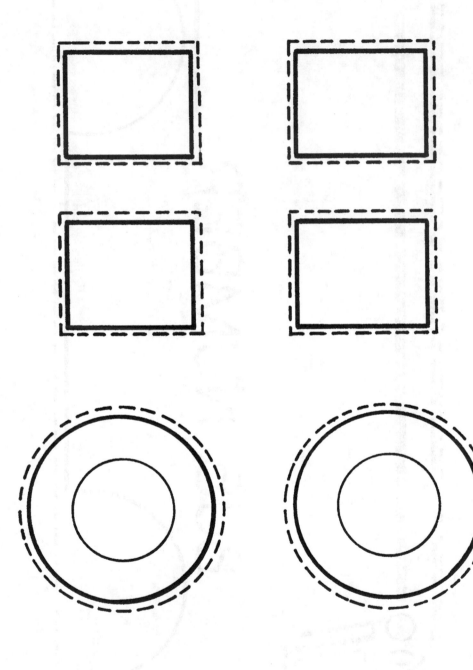

Build a Fall Scarecrow

HAT TILTED TO LEFT:
Less than 10 letters in first name when number is doubled

EYES ARE CIRCLES:
Like to drink apple juice

YELLOW SHIRT:
Born in fall

EVEN NUMBER OF PATCHES: A girl

RED PANTS:
Like to go camping

Math Skills

- counting
- geometry: shapes
- greater than/less than
- directionality: left, right
- even/odd numbers

Materials

- reproducible glyph patterns and legend from pages 17–19
- completed scarecrow glyph
- scissors
- glue or paste
- construction paper
- crayons

Creating the Glyph

Distribute copies of the scarecrow glyph patterns and the legend to students. Review the legend, one characteristic at a time as you display a glyph you have completed. Then distribute the other materials and invite students to use the legend to create their own personal scarecrow glyph. Students can glue or paste the elements of the glyph onto construction paper for a sturdy backing.

Critical Thinking

Select six of the completed scarecrow glyphs and sort them into two groups. Ask students to "Guess the Rule," by looking for the attributes that are common to all of the scarecrows in one of the groups. The attributes could be that the scarecrows have an odd number of patches (means that they are boys) or pants that are blue (means that the favorite activity would be to collect leaves). The age and grade

Literature LINKS

Picking Apples and Pumpkins by Amy and Richard Hutchings. Cartwheel Books, 1994.

This story, set on a farm, follows a family as they pick apples, have a picnic, select pumpkins, bake a pie, and carve a jack-o'lantern. An apple pie recipe is included.

When Autumn Comes by Robert Maas. Owlet Publications, 1992.

Students explore the start of the autumn season in the country through colorful photographs.

Why Do Leaves Change Colors? by Betsy Maestro. HarperTrophy Publishers, 1994.

Students learn how leaves change color and separate from the tree in autumn. The leaves are illustrated in different sizes, shapes, and colors. Activities using leaves are included.

level of your students should determine the number of attributes that are grouped together. Fewer attributes (or more obvious attributes) will make it easier for students to analyze the grouping and guess the rule.

Explore More

☀ **Language Arts** Invite students to write about their favorite things to do in the fall. Encourage them to illustrate their narratives. After each student has a chance to read his or her writing aloud to the class, compile all the pages into a "Big Book of Fall Activities" and place it in the reading corner.

☀ **Math** Use a Venn diagram to compare the characteristics of apples and pumpkins. Draw the overlapping circles and label as shown. Call on students to give a characteristic of either apples or pumpkins; as each characteristic is offered, ask the class if it belongs in the circle for apples, in the circle for pumpkins, or in the overlapping portion indicating it is a characteristic of both. Ask volunteers to summarize how apples and pumpkins are alike and different.

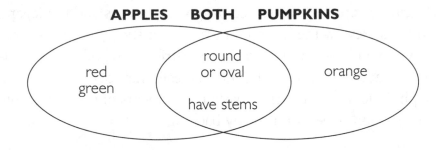

☀ **Community, Math** Visit a pumpkin patch and ask students to observe how pumpkins are grown. Or invite a farm owner to visit the classroom and talk to the class about growing, harvesting, and selling pumpkins. Then do activities with pumpkins: sort them by size or shape, count their seeds, weigh them, measure their circumference, and decorate them.

Name _____

1 Double the number of letters in your first name.
How many letters are there?

Hat	less than 10	exactly 10	more than 10
	tilt hat to the left	keep hat straight	tilt hat to the right

2 When were you born?

Color of Shirt	white	green	red	yellow
	winter	spring	summer	fall

3 What would you like to do in the fall?

Color of Pants	black	blue	red
	jump in a pile of leaves	collect colorful leaves	go camping

4 Are you a boy or a girl? Draw patches.

Patches	even number of patches	odd number of patches
	girl	boy

5 What do you like to eat or drink?

Shape of Eye	△	☐	◯
	applesauce	apple pie	apple juice

Great Glyphs Around the Year Scholastic Professional Books

18

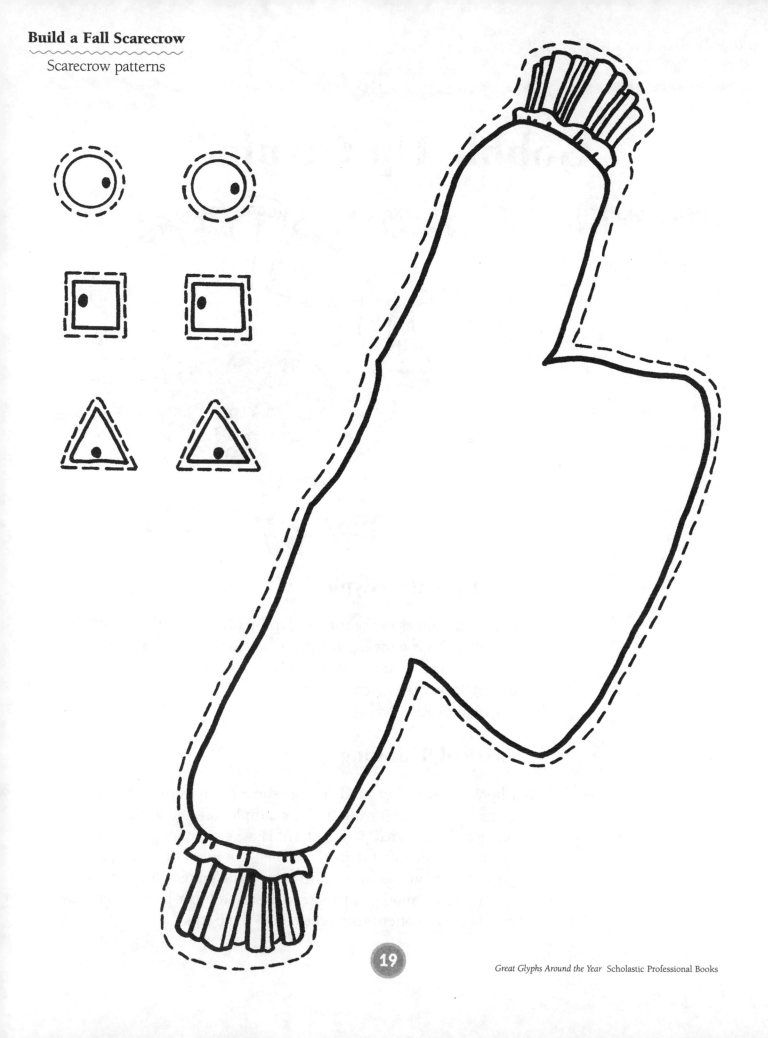

Great Glyphs Around the Year Scholastic Professional Books

Gobble Up Glyphs!

Math Skills

- patterns: recognizing, extending
- one-to-one correspondence
- counting

Materials

- reproducible glyph patterns and legend from pages 22–24
- completed turkey glyph
- scissors
- glue or paste
- crayons

FEATHERS IN AB/AB PATTERN: 4 people

ORANGE WATTLE: Have seen parade in person

TAN BODY: Going away for Thanksgiving

PURPLE WING: Pie is favorite food

ORANGE FEET: Will eat dinner far away

Creating the Glyph

Distribute copies of the turkey glyph patterns and the legend to students. Review the legend, one characteristic at a time, as you display a turkey you have completed. Then distribute the other materials. Invite students to use the legend to create their own personal turkey glyph.

Critical Thinking

Choose one attribute and arrange some of the completed turkey glyphs in an AB/AB pattern. For example, use the wattle and make a red/pink/red/pink pattern. Have students look at the glyphs and identify the pattern. Then ask them to select a turkey glyph that would come next to extend the pattern. Repeat the activity using another attribute to create another pattern, such as an ABC/ABC pattern using the color of the feet.

Explore More

☀ **Math** Ask students to collect information from family members about their favorite foods to eat at Thanksgiving. Then create bar graphs or pictographs to represent their findings. To limit the variations that need to be depicted on the graph, you might brainstorm a list of five or six items with the class and then have them limit choices to those items.

☀ **Math, Language Arts** Bring in a simple recipe for stuffing or cranberry sauce and use it with the class. Help students read the recipe, practice measuring ingredients, and increase the amount of the recipe if necessary to feed the entire class. After the cooking and eating, have students write a sequence story explaining the steps of the process.

☀ **Math** Have students compare the number of letters in their first and last names. Have students use the name that has more letters, make that number of feathers, and use this quantity of feathers to make a pattern. For example, if a student's name has eight letters, he or she would make a pattern using eight feathers.

Literature LINKS

All About Turkeys by Jim Arnosky. Scholastic Books, 1998.
This book includes information about turkeys' habitats, behavior, life cycle, and physical characteristics.

Thanksgiving at the Tappletons by Eileen Spinelli. HarperTrophy, 1982.
Mrs. Tappleton wakes up early on Thanksgiving Day to prepare the holiday meal. She assigns family members different jobs to help her. However, each member of the family encounters a different problem, which they must resolve before the relatives arrive.

'Twas the Night Before Thanksgiving by Dav Pilkey. Scholastic Books, 1990.
Eight children board a bus to visit a turkey farm the day before Thanksgiving. When they learn the fate of the turkeys, the children devise a plan to help them escape.

1 What are your Thanksgiving plans?

Color of Body	**tan**	**brown**
	I am going away.	I am not going away.

2 How many people live in your home?
Use six feathers. Color them to make a pattern.

Pattern of Feathers	**AB/AB pattern**	**AAB/AAB pattern**	**ABC/ABC pattern**
	exactly four people	more than four people	fewer than four people

3 Where will you eat your Thanksgiving meal?

Color of Feet	**orange**	**pink**	**red**
	far away	at my house	near my house

4 Have you seen a Thanksgiving parade?

Color of Wattle	**red**	**orange**	**pink**
	yes, on television	yes, in person	no

5 What is your favorite Thanksgiving food?

Color of Wing	**brown**	**purple**	**black**	**yellow**
	stuffing	pie	turkey	other

22

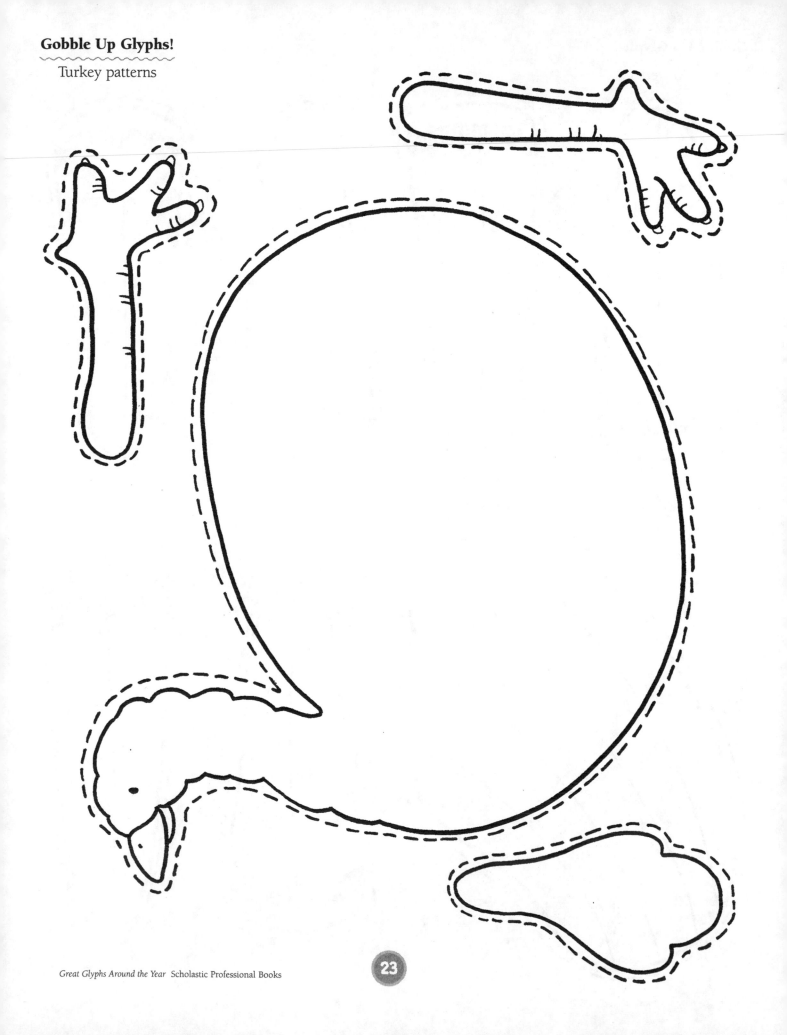

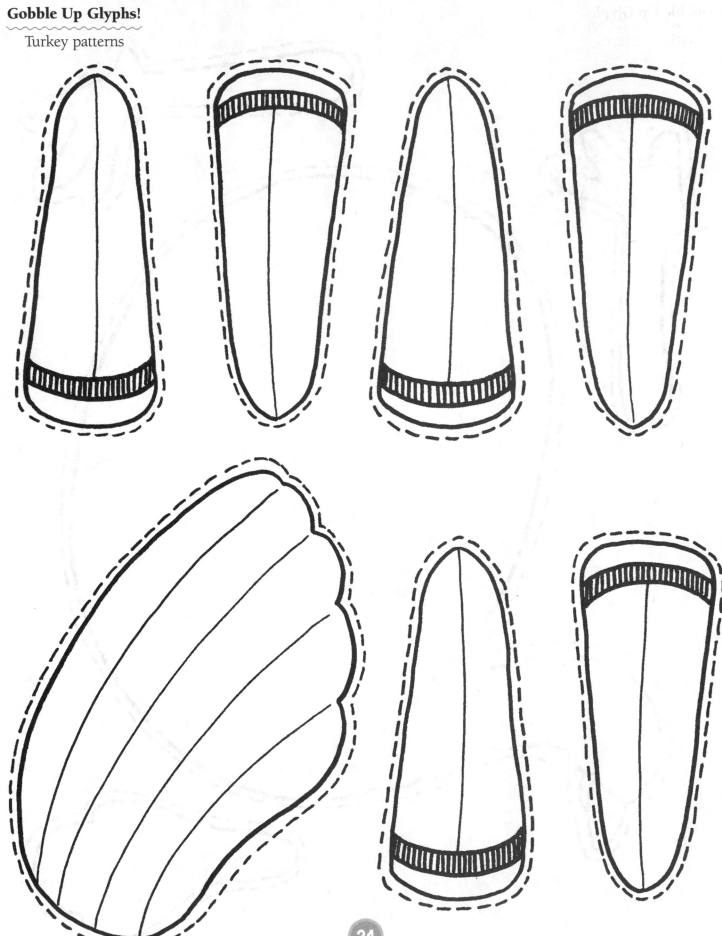

Gingerbread Cookies—Yum!

YELLOW COOKIE:
Sugar cookie tastes best

EYES ARE TRIANGLES:
6 letters in first name

PURPLE MOUTH:
Like eating warm cookies

FOUR BUTTONS:
Eat 4 cookies

BELT: Like chocolate
milk best

Math Skills

- geometry: shapes
- one-to-one correspondence
- greater than/less than/ equal to
- counting
- addition, subtraction

Materials

- reproducible glyph patterns and legend from pages 27–29
- completed gingerbread glyph
- scissors
- glue or paste
- crayons

Creating the Glyph

Distribute copies of the gingerbread cookie glyph patterns and the legend to students. Review the legend, one characteristic at a time, as you display a cookie glyph you have completed. Then distribute the other materials, and invite students to create their own personal gingerbread cookie glyph.

Critical Thinking

Ask students to display their completed cookie glyphs. Then ask them to form three groups: those with brown cookies, those with tan, and those with yellow. Collect the glyphs from each group. Create a large wall graph by making rows of cookies of each color. Discuss what the graph shows. Ask questions such as:

☼ How many children in our class like chocolate cookies best?

☼ How many more like chocolate than sugar cookies?

☼ How many like sugar and gingerbread?

Explore More

☼ **Home/School, Math, Language Arts** Have children collect data from members of their family to determine which of the following is their favorite type of cookie: sugar, peanut butter, chocolate chip, or gingerbread. Once everyone has brought in this information, decide on a way to graph the data. For example, students could make a bar graph with a bar to represent each of the four types of cookies. Then have students make observations about the data that has been collected. Older students can write about their observations.

☼ **Math** Bring in a bag of chocolate chip cookies and give each student a cookie. (Try to find the bag that claims to have 1000 chips.) Ask students to look at their cookie and estimate how many chips it has. Develop a range based on the number of chips estimated. Then have students break their cookies apart and count the chips. Ask each student to find a way to represent on paper the number of chips their cookie had. For example, students might write the number, draw a circle for each chip, draw a cookie with dots to represent the number of chips, use tallies, and so on. Then invite students to eat their cookies.

☼ **Language Arts** Read the story "The Gingerbread Man." Find different versions of this classic tale, and compare them. Then invite students to write their own tale of a gingerbread boy or girl. Ask students to incorporate numbers in their stories.

☼ **Math** Make gingerbread cookies with the class. Sequence the steps for baking cookies. Calculate how many times the recipe must be increased in order to make enough cookies for your class. Have students do the measuring, bake, and enjoy!

☼ **Math** Use the gingerbread cookie pattern. Have students make a gingerbread boy or girl and then use their "cookies" as a nonstandard unit to measure classroom objects and distances. For example, students can measure the length and width of their desk or tabletops, the length of a bulletin board, the distance from the front to the back of the classroom, and so on.

1 What kind of cookie tastes best?

Color of Cookie	**brown**	**tan**	**yellow**
	chocolate	gingerbread	sugar

2 What flavor milk do you like with cookies?

Pattern on Belt			
	chocolate	plain	strawberry

3 How many cookies do you eat for a snack?

Number of Buttons	**0**	**1**	**2**	**3**	**4**	**5**
	none	one	two	three	four	five

4 How many letters are in your first name?

Shape of Eyes			
	exactly six	fewer than six	more than six

5 What is the best part of making cookies?

Color of Mouth	**red**	**pink**	**purple**
	measuring and stirring	tasting the batter	eating warm cookies

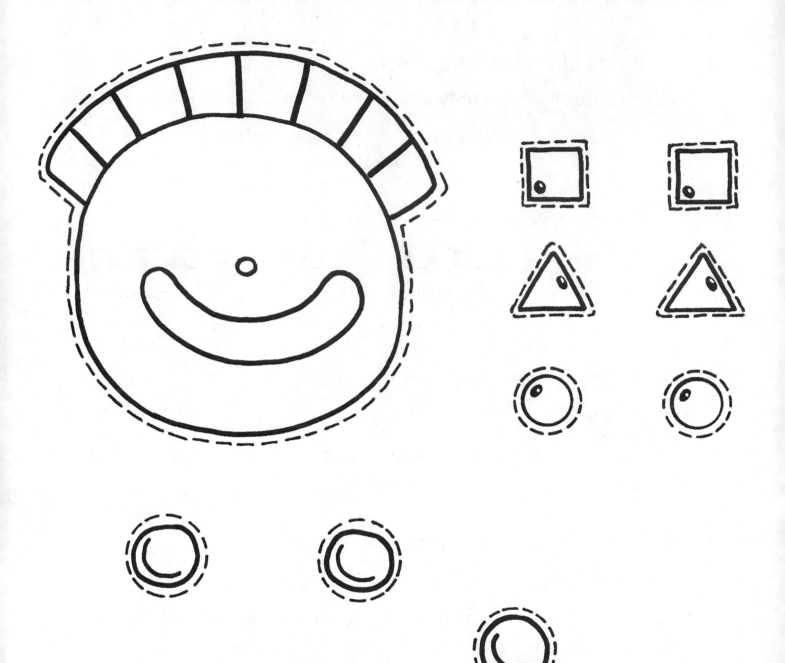

Gingerbread patterns

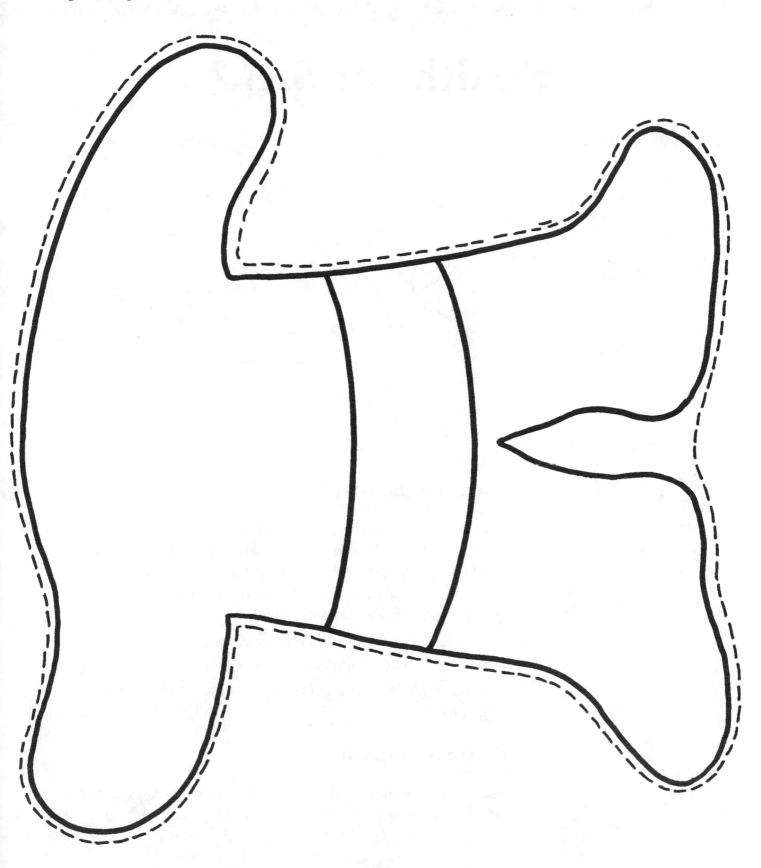

Healthy or Sick?

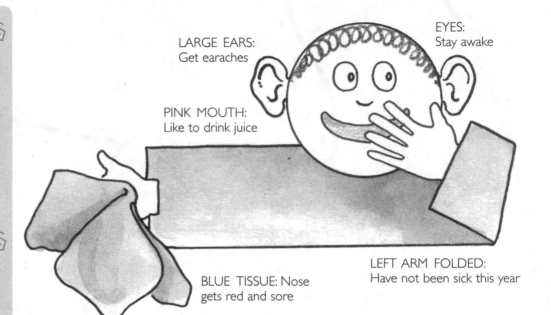

LARGE EARS: Get earaches

EYES: Stay awake

PINK MOUTH: Like to drink juice

BLUE TISSUE: Nose gets red and sore

LEFT ARM FOLDED: Have not been sick this year

Creating the Glyph

Distribute copies of the glyph patterns and the legend to students. Review the legend, one characteristic at a time, as you display a glyph you have completed. Then distribute the other materials, and invite students to use the legend to create their own personal "healthy or sick" glyph.

1. To create this glyph, students begin with a 4- by 16-inch piece of construction paper.

2. Invite students to add details such as hair to their completed glyphs.

Critical Thinking

Ask students if they think more boys or more girls get earaches when they are sick. After they make predictions, work with stu-

dents to create a method that will help answer the question, at least for the students in your classroom.

One way is to create with string two large circles on the classroom floor. One circle should be labeled "boys" and the other "girls." Have each student place his or her glyph inside one circle or the other. Once glyphs are placed, students can discuss the data and interpret the results. For example, in the "girls" circle students can count the number of people who get earaches and the number who do not by observing the size of the ears. Students can compare these numbers with the number who do and do not get earaches in the "boys" circle.

Literature LINKS

Germs Make Me Sick! by Melvin Berger. HarperCollins Publishers, 1995.
Students learn how viruses and bacteria can make us sick, how to prevent illness, and how the body fights back when germs attack.

Explore More

☼ **Math** Ask students to write number sentences based on the glyphs that have been made. For example, students could look at the number of glyphs that have open eyes plus the number of glyphs that have small ears. A number sentence and a sum could be determined. You may also give students a number sentence with missing addends, such as __ + __ = 9, and ask them to figure out which glyphs you were looking at to determine the number sentence.

☼ **Health** Invite the school nurse to visit your classroom and instruct students in good health habits to avoid catching colds and to stay healthy. Have children discuss with the nurse how germs can be spread in the classroom—and ways of preventing this and protecting themselves.

Name _____

1 What do you do when you are sick?

Eyes	⊙⊙	⊝⊝	◯◯
	stay awake	take naps	sleep all day

2 What do you like to drink when you are sick?

Color of Mouth	**pink**	**red**	**tan**	**orange**
	juice	ginger ale or soda	hot chocolate	something else

3 Do you get earaches when you are sick?

Size of Ears	**large ears**	**small ears**
	yes	no

4 Have you have been sick during this school year?

Arms	**right arm folded toward face**	**left arm folded toward face**
	yes	no

5 What happens to your nose when you have a cold?

Color of Tissue	**blue**	**white**
	My nose gets red and sore.	My nose gets runny or stuffy.

Great Glyphs Around the Year Scholastic Professional Books

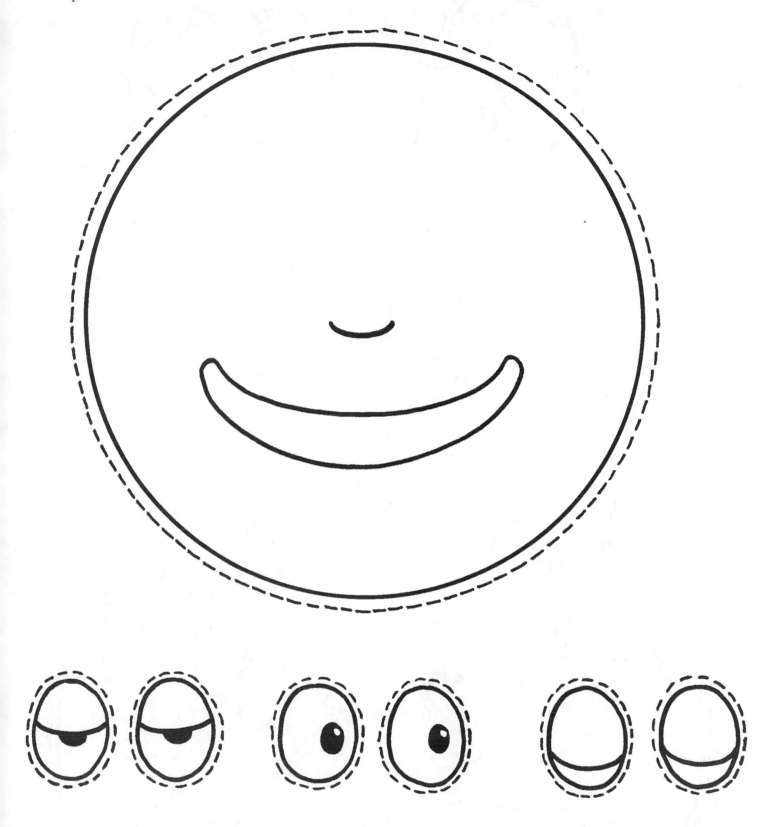

Great Glyphs Around the Year Scholastic Professional Books

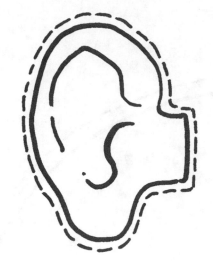
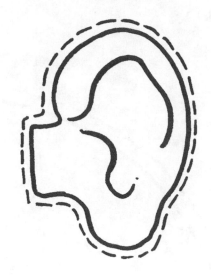
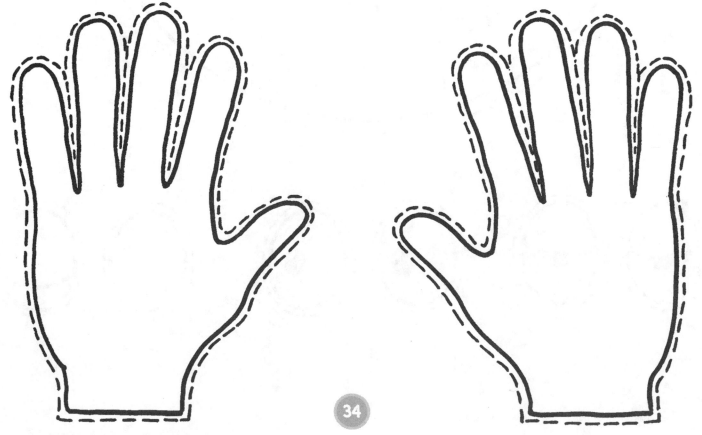

My Coins Go Jingle-Jangle

Math Skills

- directionality: left, right; above, below
- writing numbers
- money: value of coins, combinations of coins to represent a given value
- addition

Materials

- reproducible coin patterns and legend from pages 37–39
- completed coin glyph
- scissors
- glue or paste
- crayons
- real or play money (optional)

YELLOW COIN: A girl

TOWN: Somerville

GEORGE WASHINGTON: Born in Fall or Winter

SIX(6): 6 years old

THREE STARS: 3 people in family

YEAR BORN: 1994

Creating the Glyph

Distribute copies of the coin glyph patterns and the legend to students. Review the legend, one characteristic at a time, as you display a glyph you have completed. Then distribute the other materials, and invite students to use the legend to create their own personal coin glyph.

Critical Thinking

Choose a group of student glyphs randomly. Have students identify the total value represented by the quarters and pennies used in the glyphs. Once they have found the total, ask them to find another combination of real or play coins to show that same amount. For example, if the total for five students' glyphs was

53¢ (2 quarters, 3 pennies) this amount may be shown in a variety of other ways:

☀ 1 quarter, 28 pennies

☀ 1 quarter, 2 dimes, 1 nickel, 3 pennies

☀ 1 quarter, 1 dime, 3 nickels, 3 pennies

There are many more ways to represent the amount. You can challenge students to find a specific way, such as the way that uses the greatest number of coins; the way that uses the least number; the way that uses only dimes and pennies; and so on. Repeat the activity several times using different glyphs each time.

Explore More

☀ **Math** Ask students to use coins to represent the date on the calendar. For example, the 21st of the month could be shown with two dimes and one penny, or with four nickels and one penny. Have students work in small groups, and assign each group a date. Ask them to make the "value" of their date in as many ways as they can. Then invite a member of each group to report their findings to the class.

☀ **Math** Provide pairs of students with a penny each, and have them conduct a probability experiment. First, ask students to guess what the chance is of getting "heads" if they flip a coin. Then, ask them to flip the coin, recording with tallies the number of times the coin lands on "heads" and "tails" in a set of 10 flips. Ask them to try again and record the results of 20 flips of the coin, and again with 30 flips. Discuss the results. Did the results change depending on the number of flips?

☀ **Career Awareness, Math** Take the class on a field trip to a bank or invite someone who works in a bank to visit your class. Ask a bank employee to tell the class about his or her job, including how he or she uses math on the job.

Literature LINKS

Benny's Pennies by Pat Brisson. Bantam Doubleday Dell, 1993.

A young boy gets advice from his family about how to spend his five pennies. Readers can keep track of how many pennies he has spent and how many remain after each purchase.

Bunny Money by Rosemary Wells. Dial Books for Young Readers, 1997.

Ruby has saved a wallet full of money to buy her grandmother a birthday present. She goes shopping looking for just the right gift.

Let's Find Out About Money by Kathy Barabas. Scholastic, 1997.

Readers are taken on a journey that describes the process of making money. A map at the end of the story shows the entire process in a simple, clear way.

Name _____ **My Coins Go Jingle-Jangle**

1 In what season were you born?

Choice of Coin	George Washington	Abraham Lincoln
	Fall or Winter	Spring or Summer

2 Write the year you were born below the president.

3 Write the name of the town or city you live in above the president's head.

4 Are you a boy or a girl?

Color of Coin	orange	yellow
	boy	girl

5 How many people are in your family? Paste stars on the left side of the coin.

Number of Stars	2 stars	3 stars	4 stars	5 stars
	two	three	four	five or more

6 Write the word and numeral for your age on the right side of your coin.

Great Glyphs Around the Year Scholastic Professional Books

Come Fly With Me!

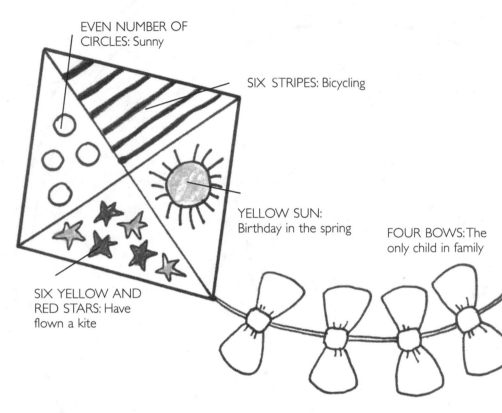

EVEN NUMBER OF CIRCLES: Sunny

SIX STRIPES: Bicycling

YELLOW SUN: Birthday in the spring

FOUR BOWS: The only child in family

SIX YELLOW AND RED STARS: Have flown a kite

Math Skills

◆ geometry: vertical, horizontal lines; shapes
◆ even/odd numbers
◆ one-to-one correspondence
◆ directionality: left, right; top, bottom
◆ addition
◆ fractions

Materials

◆ reproducible glyph patterns and legend from pages 42–43
◆ completed kite glyph
◆ tape
◆ scissors
◆ pieces of string cut to 6 inches
◆ crayons
◆ ruler

Creating the Glyph

Distribute copies of the kite glyph patterns and the legend to students. Review the legend, one characteristic at a time, as you display a glyph you have completed. Then distribute the other materials, and invite students to use the legend to create their own personal kite glyph.

1. To begin, have students use a ruler to draw a line from top to bottom, and from left to right, to divide the kite into four equal parts.

2. Have students identify the shapes they made. (*triangles*) Discuss that each triangle is one quarter of the whole quadrilateral.

3. Students can use tape to attach the string to the kite and bows onto the string as they complete step 5 of the legend.

Literature LINKS

Catch the Wind—All About Kites by Gail Gibbons. Little, Brown and Company, 1995.

Gail Gibbons presents a survey of the five basic types of kites. The book also includes information about the history, construction, and uses of kites. Instructions for making a kite are provided.

Curious George Flies a Kite by Margaret Rey. Houghton Mifflin Publishers, 1958.

Curious George meets a man with a kite who teaches him how to fly it.

The Emperor and the Kite by Jane Yolen. Putnam Publisher Group, 1988. (Caldecott Award Winner)

A Chinese emperor's youngest daughter spends her days playing with a kite made from paper and sticks.

A Sky Full of Kites by Osmond Molarsky. Tricycle Press, 1996.

A young boy paints such a large picture that he is unable to find a place to display it. He finally turns the painting into a kite.

Critical Thinking

Ask students what part of the kite glyph they should look at to identify everyone's favorite springtime activity. (*the upper right*) Gather students' ideas about how they could make a graph that would represent this information. Then divide the class in small groups. Ask some groups to make a vertical bar graph and the others to make a horizontal bar graph. Discuss how both types represent the same data.

Explore More

☼ **Math** Ask students to write equations that match the number of stars and stripes they drew. For example, six stars and two stripes: $6 + 2 = 8$.

☼ **Language Arts** Invite students to review the springtime activities they represented on their kite glyphs. Then discuss other favorite springtime activities, and make a class list. Ask each student to choose an activity and write about it, telling why they like (or would like) to do it.

☼ **Science, Art** If your school has an art teacher, ask him or her to make kites with students. Students can fly their kites, identify those that fly better than others, and analyze what makes one kite fly better than another. A store-bought kite could be purchased and compared to the students' handmade kites to identify similarities and differences and to compare which flies better.

☼ **Math, Science** Have students make another kite. To figure out how long a tail the kite can have, ask each student to place a bottle cap at a starting line on a table or desk. (All students should use the same starting line.) Give a straw to each student, and invite students, one at a time, to blow once through the straw to move the bottle cap along the table. Each student should then measure the distance his or her cap traveled, and cut a piece of string the same length for the kite's tail.

Name _____ **Come Fly With Me!**

1 What is your favorite springtime weather? Draw shapes.

Top left part of the kite	even number of circles	odd number of triangles	even number of squares	odd number of rectangles
	sunny	rainy	windy	snowy

2 Which outdoor activity would you like to try? Draw stripes.

Top right part of the kite	fewer than 5	more than 4 but fewer than 8	8	more than 8 but fewer than 11
	flying a kite	bicycling	skate-boarding	play a team sport

3 Have you ever flown a kite? Draw six stars in all.

Bottom left part of the kite	6 yellow and red stars	6 blue and green stars
	yes	no

4 When is your birthday? Draw a sun.

Bottom right part of the kite	yellow	orange
	in the spring	not in the spring

5 What position are you in your family?

Number of Bows	1	2	3	4
	youngest child	oldest child	a middle child	the only child

Great Glyphs Around the Year Scholastic Professional Books

Come Fly With Me!

Kite pattern

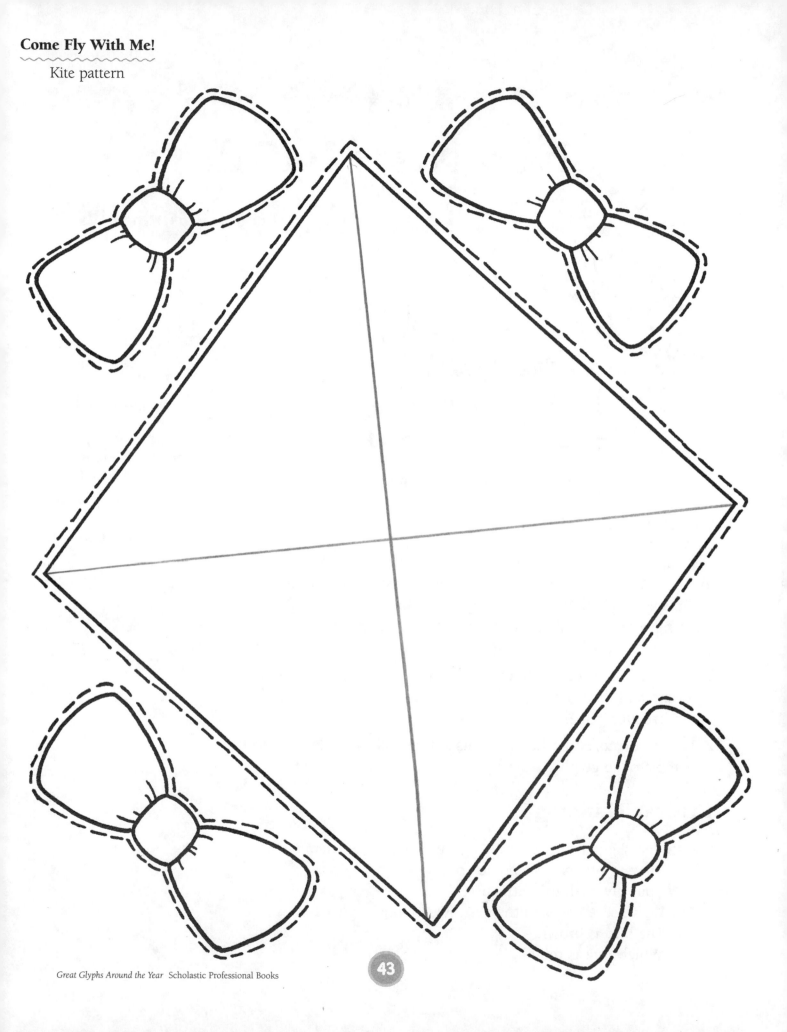

43

New Nests for All

BIRD IN NEST:
Have seen a
bird eating

EVEN NUMBER OF EGGS:
Age is an even number

CRACKS ON
TWO EGGS:
Never saw an
egg hatch

RED BIRD: Born in
a different country

BRANCH POINTING RIGHT:
Have never seen a nest

Math Skills

◆ counting
◆ directionality: left,
right
◆ even/odd numbers
◆ position: inside,
outside

Materials

◆ reproducible glyph
patterns and legend
from pages 46–48
◆ completed bird's nest
glyph
◆ construction paper
◆ scissors
◆ glue or paste
◆ crayons

Creating the Glyph

Distribute copies of the bird's nest glyph patterns and the legend
to students. Review the legend, one characteristic at a time, as
you display a glyph you have completed. Then distribute the
other materials, and invite students to use the legend to create
their own personal bird's nest glyph.

1. Tell students to begin by answering the first question on the
legend and then pasting the branch and the nest on a sheet of
construction paper.

2. Have students add other elements as they follow the legend to
complete the glyph.

Critical Thinking

Use students' glyphs to generate logic problems. For example:
     I have a branch that points to the left.
     I put my bird inside the nest.
     I have seven eggs in the nest. (One has a crack.)
     The bird is brown.
     Which nest is mine?

Then progress to higher-order thinking problems, such as:

> I am seven years old and was born in Korea.
> I have never seen an egg hatch.
> But I have seen a bird eating and a nest in a tree.
> Which nest is mine?

Explore More

☼ **Science** Invite students to research different types of animals whose young hatch from eggs. Most students will realize, for example, that birds lay eggs. Challenge them to discover which other animals do (*many amphibians, reptiles, and even a few mammals*). Ask students to find out how these animals are similar and how they are different.

☼ **Physical Education, Math** Have students complete a survey of their schoolmates to determine the different springtime sports that students participate in. They can poll students in their own and other classrooms and then make a graphic representation to show the data, using pictographs or bar graphs.

☼ **Math, Science** Help students keep a record of daily temperatures during the months of April and May using an outdoor thermometer or the daily high temperature reported in a newspaper or television news show. If students are tracking the temperature themselves, it is important to record the temperature at the same time each day. Have a volunteer record the daily temperature on a chart; create a line graph from the data that will show how the temperature changes from day to day. Ask students to predict how the line should look from beginning to end. (*It should go from lower numbers at the left to higher numbers at the right, showing an overall warming trend.*)

Name _____

1 Have you ever seen a nest in a tree?

Direction of Branch	**pointing to the left**	**pointing to the right**
	yes	no

2 Have you ever seen a bird eating?

Position of Bird	**inside the nest**	**on the branch**
	yes	no

3 How old are you?

Number of Eggs in Nest	**even number of eggs in the nest**	**odd number of eggs in the nest**
	my age is an even number	my age is an odd number

4 Have you ever seen an egg hatch? Draw cracks.

Cracks in Eggs	**crack in one egg**	**cracks in two eggs**
	yes	no

5 Where were you born?

Color of Bird	**blue**	**brown**	**red**
	in the state where I live now	in a different state from where I live now	in a different country from where I live now

Great Glyphs Around the Year Scholastic Professional Books

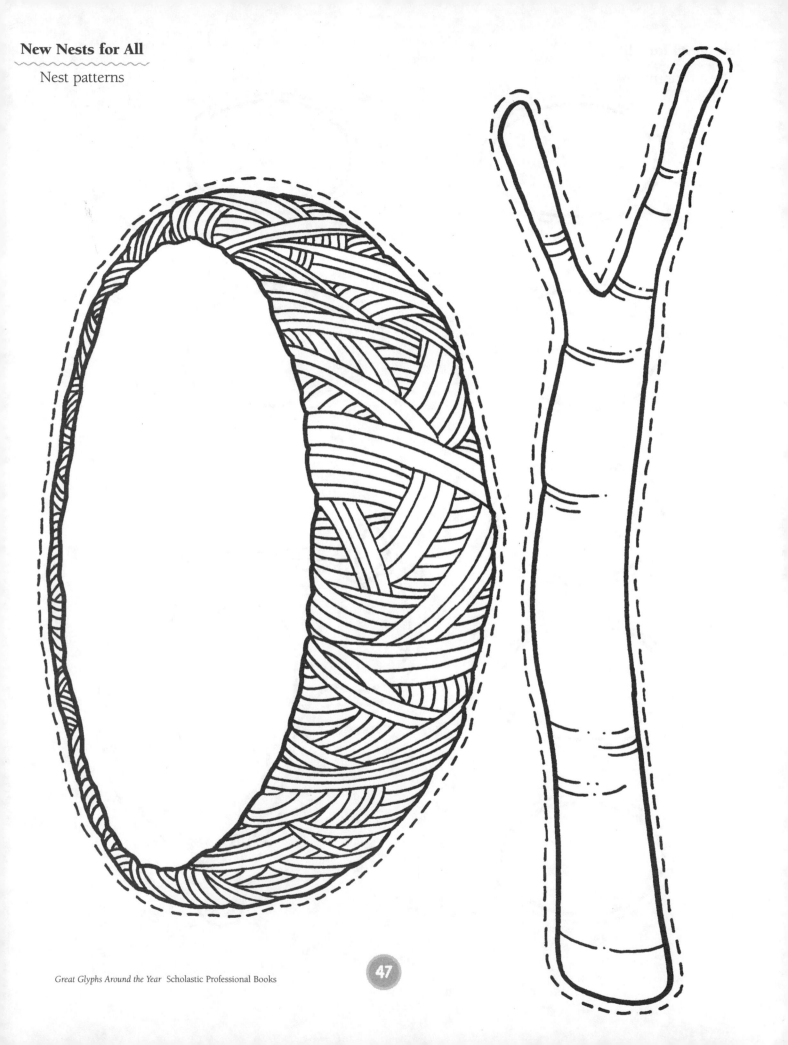

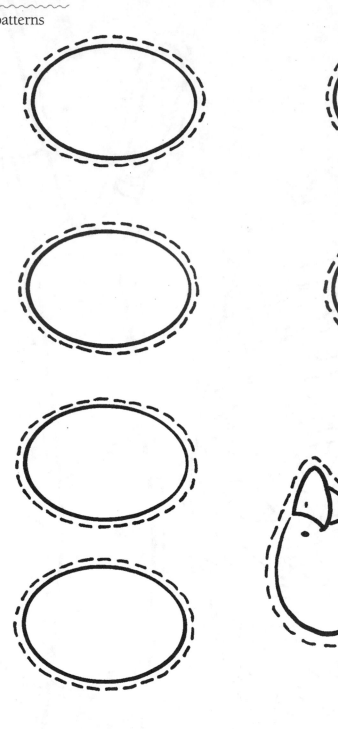

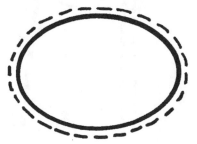

Great Glyphs Around the Year Scholastic Professional Books

Flowers Spring Up Everywhere!

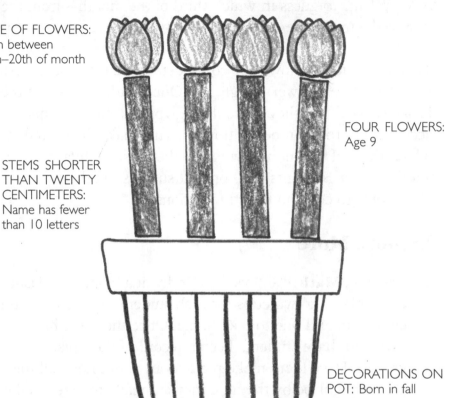

TYPE OF FLOWERS: Born between 11th–20th of month

STEMS SHORTER THAN TWENTY CENTIMETERS: Name has fewer than 10 letters

FOUR FLOWERS: Age 9

DECORATIONS ON POT: Born in fall

Creating the Glyph

Distribute copies of the flower pot glyph patterns and the legend to students. Review the legend, one characteristic at a time, as you display a glyph you have completed. Then distribute the other materials, and invite students to use the legend to create their own personal flower pot glyph.

1. Tell students to paste all the elements of their glyph onto construction paper for a sturdy backing.

2. Help students measure the flower stems with centimeter rulers. They can cut one stem and then make additional stems of the same length for the number of flowers they need. As students paste the elements of the glyph onto construction paper, tell them to paste the flower stems carefully so that the full length of each stem is visible.

Critical Thinking

Ask students to guess in which third of the month—from the first to the tenth; the eleventh to the twentieth; or the twenty-first to the end of the month—most students have birthdays. Then ask students how they could determine this exactly, using their completed flower pot glyphs. Once students present their ideas, suggest that they place their glyphs in three groups according to the number of flowers. Then have them predict which third of the month will have the most birthdays in another class. Students can conduct surveys in other classrooms to confirm their predictions.

Explore More

☼ **Science, Math** Plant seeds in individual paper or plastic cups, planting two cups for each student: one to keep in the classroom and one to take home. Once the seeds have sprouted, have students keep a record of their plants' growth. Have them make predictions about how tall the plants might be by the time they are ready to take one home to give to their mothers for a Mother's Day gift. Continue to observe and measure the plants that remain in the classroom. Students can chart and graph data that show their growth, conduct experiments to see how light and water affect growth, and so on.

☼ **Science** Take a field trip to a local nature center or nursery to help students learn about different kinds of plants and flowers that grow in your part of the country. Request that an employee talk with the class about how local plants grow and are cared for.

Literature LINKS

Flower Garden by Eve Bunting. Harcourt Brace, 1994.
A young girl and her father plan a flower garden to surprise her mother. Five common flowers are identified.

The Reason for a Flower by Ruth Heller. Price Stern Sloan, 1983.
This charming book, written in rhyme, explains plant reproduction and the role of a plant's flowers.

Name _____   **Flowers Spring Up Everywhere!**

(1) In what season were you born?

Decorations on Flower Pot				
	spring	summer	fall	winter

(2) How old are you?

Number of Flowers in Pot	1	2	3	4
	six	seven	eight	nine

(3) How many letters are in your first and last name combined?

Height of Flower Stems	**shorter than 20 centimeters**	**20 centimeters tall**	**taller than 20 centimeters**
	fewer than 10 letters	exactly 10 letters	more than 10 letters

(4) Where in the month does your birthday come?

Type of Flowers			
	1st–10th	11th–20th	21st–31st

51

Flower patterns

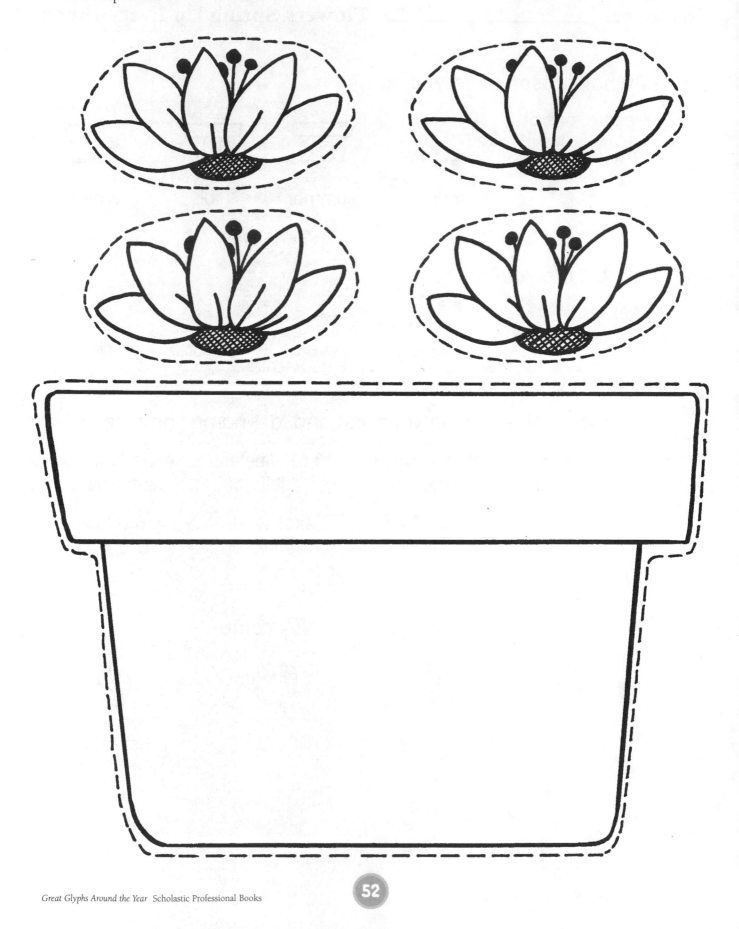

Flowers Spring Up Everywhere!

Flower patterns

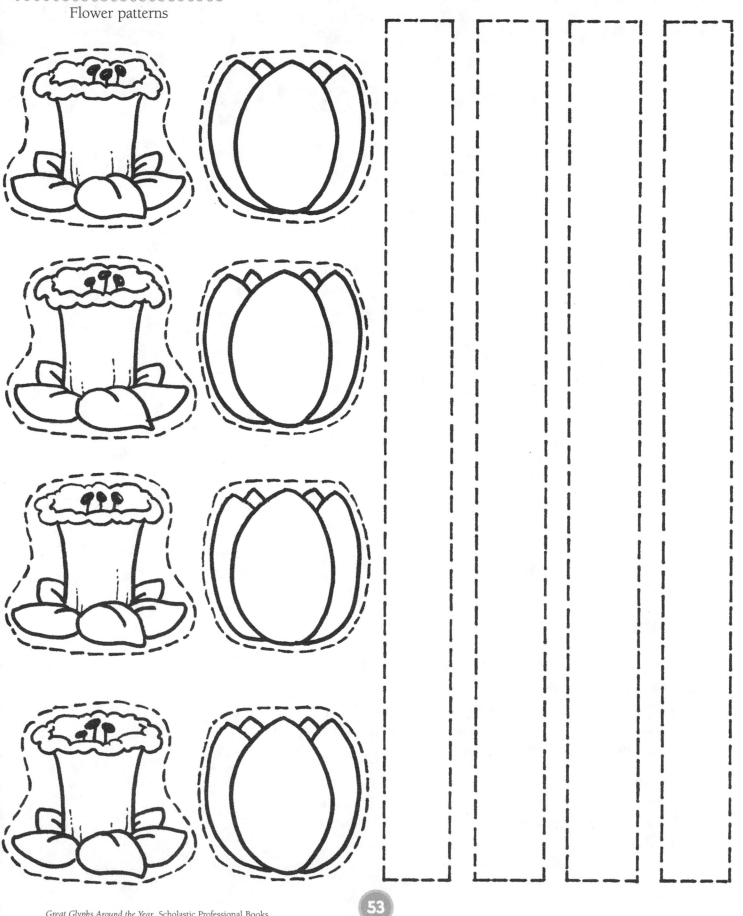

Graduation Day

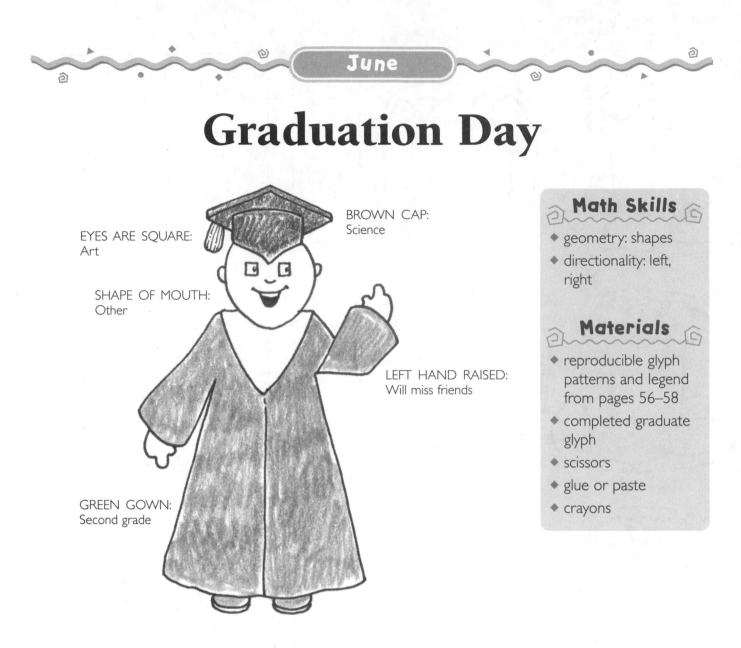

EYES ARE SQUARE:
Art

SHAPE OF MOUTH:
Other

GREEN GOWN:
Second grade

BROWN CAP:
Science

LEFT HAND RAISED:
Will miss friends

Math Skills

- geometry: shapes
- directionality: left, right

Materials

- reproducible glyph patterns and legend from pages 56–58
- completed graduate glyph
- scissors
- glue or paste
- crayons

Creating the Glyph

Distribute copies of the graduate glyph patterns and the legend to students. Review the legend, one characteristic at a time, as you display a glyph you have completed. Then distribute the other materials, and invite students to use the legend to create their own personal graduate glyph.

This glyph works nicely for students who are "graduating" from the primary school to the intermediate school. It may also be used with any other grade with some adjusting of responses. Adjust the legend as necessary.

The Gator Girls by Joanna Cole. William Morrow and Company, 1995.

Two best friends plan a summer of fun. Then one gets sent to summer camp. The two friends find ways to overcome the situation, and come to understand the true meaning of friendship.

Grandma Summer by Harley Jessup. Viking Children's Books, 1999.

A young boy spends his summer with his grandmother at the beach. His doubts about staying vanish as he enjoys the special experience.

The Great Summer Camp Catastrophe by Jean Van Leeuwen. Dial Books, 1992.

Three city mice, living in a dollhouse in a large department store, are accidentally boxed up and shipped to a boy at summer camp.

Critical Thinking

Play a game of "ten questions" with the class. Post all the completed glyphs on a bulletin board or elsewhere around the classroom. Have students take turns picking a "secret" glyph and giving clues to their choice based on characteristics that are displayed. The rest of the class must guess the secret glyph in ten guesses or fewer. For example:

☼ The glyph I chose shows the favorite subject was math.

☼ It shows the person began attending our school in first grade.

As each clue is revealed, the class can gather some glyphs that fit the clue and eliminate others.

Explore More

☼ **Math, Language Arts** Ask students to talk about people that they know who have graduated. Have students determine how old they will be when they graduate from high school. Ask them to figure out what year it will be when they graduate. Then invite students to write about something they might do when they graduate from high school.

☼ **Language Arts, Home/School** Staple together several pieces of lined notebook paper for each student. Have them make autograph books and allow them time to exchange signatures. You might include a class list of addresses and encourage students to be "pen pals" during the summer. (Before distributing addresses, be sure to obtain permission from parents or caregivers.)

☼ **Language Arts** Invite students to write about their dream vacation. Ask them to include where they would go, what they would like to do, and why. When writing is complete, invite volunteers to read their dream vacation stories to the class.

Name _____

1 When did you begin attending this school?

Color of Gown	blue	red	green	purple
	kindergarten	first grade	second grade	third grade

2 What was your favorite subject this year?

Color of Cap	black	yellow	brown	orange
	math	reading	science	other

3 What was your favorite "special" class this year?

Shape of Eyes				
	art	music	physical education	other

4 How do you feel about leaving this grade? Draw a mouth.

Shape of Mouth				
	happy	sad	nervous	other

5 What will you miss most about this grade?

Which Hand is Raised	left	right
	my friends	my teacher

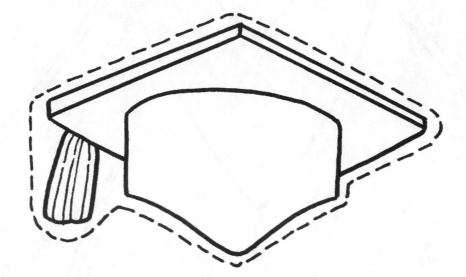

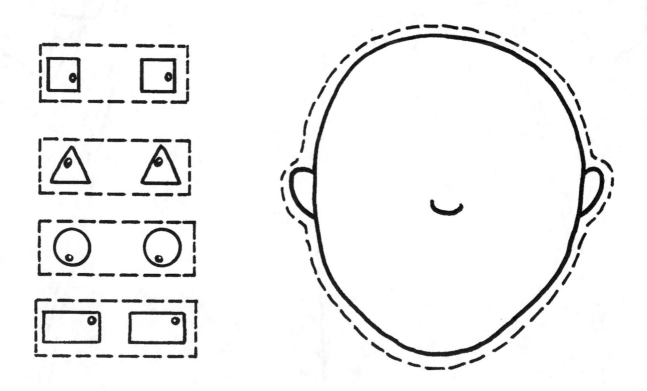

Great Glyphs Around the Year Scholastic Professional Books

Make a Summertime Splash!

KIDNEY-SHAPED POOL: Like to swim

ORANGE RAFT: Like to swim in ocean

RED AND WHITE INNERTUBE: Like to swim in backyard pool

FOUR FLOATS: Like to swim in shallow end

Creating the Glyph

Distribute copies of the swimming pool glyph patterns and the legend to students. Review the legend, one characteristic at a time, as you display a glyph you have completed. Then distribute the other materials, and invite students to use the legend to create their own personal swimming pool glyph.

1. Use blue construction paper to form the "pool." Students can cut the shape they need according to the legend.

2. Help students to cut yarn or string to reach across their pools. Help them tape it in place to form the "rope" for floats in step 4 of the legend.

Critical Thinking

Students use the color of their rafts to indicate where they would most like to swim. Here is another way to collect and represent this information.

1. Use four two-liter bottles and label each one with a different place to swim. One bottle should be "ocean," another "lake,"

the third "swimming pool," and the last "I do not like to swim." Place a funnel in each bottle.

2. Add blue food coloring to a large container of water.

3. Have each student in turn fill a 1/4 cup container with the blue water and pour it into the bottle that is labeled with the place where they would like to swim.

4. Once all students have had a turn, ask questions such as those that follow about the height of the water in each of the bottles.

☼ What can we tell about the people in this class based on the data that we have collected?

☼ How many people do you think poured the water in the "lake" bottle? the "pool" bottle? the "ocean" bottle? How do you know this? How can we figure out the number?

☼ Would the bottles look the same if we did this experiment in another classroom? Why do you think this?

☼ If we added the water from one bottle to another do you think the water would reach the top of the bottle? Why or why not?

Explore More

☼ **Health, Physical Education** Take a field trip to a local pool, or invite a trained lifeguard to visit your classroom. Ask the lifeguard to discuss pool safety, including how people are expected to behave in and around the pool, diving safety, and how the lifeguards keep the water in the pool clean and safe for swimming.

☼ **Math** Construct a Venn diagram to compare swimming in a lake, a pool, and the ocean. Draw three circles that overlap in the center. Label each one: lake, ocean, pool. Invite students who have experienced swimming in each type of water to make statements about the experience (or make statements about why they would prefer one over the other), and record the information in the appropriate circle. Ask students to summarize the information from the visual representations. Discuss what the information in the center represents.

Literature LINKS

Cannonball Chris by Jean Marzollo. Demco Media, 1987.
A second grader who is the biggest and funniest child in his class is afraid of deep water. His father helps him overcome his fear and the boy wins a prize for diving.

Froggy Learns to Swim by Jonathan London. Viking Children's Books, 1995.
Froggy is afraid to learn to swim, but his mother knows just how to help him overcome his fear.

Get Set! Swim! by Jeannine Atkins. Lee and Low Books, 1998.
A young girl and her brother are off to the suburbs to swim at a meet. Although her school loses the meet, the girl learns the value of team spirit.

Swim by Eve Rice. Greenwillow Press, 1996.
This story presents a simple, realistic view of what it is like when a child learns to swim.

Name _____

1 How do you feel about swimming?

Shape of Pool	▭	🫘	⬭	◯
	I love to swim.	I like to swim.	I do not like to swim.	I have never been swimming.

2 Where would you rather swim?

Color of Raft	**red**	**orange**	**green**	**yellow**
	pool	ocean	lake	I do not like to swim.

3 What type of pool would you like to swim in?

Color of Innertube	**red and white**	**black and white**
	a backyard pool	a neighborhood pool

4 Where do you like to swim?

Number of Floats on Rope	**5**	**4**
	in the deep end	in the shallow end

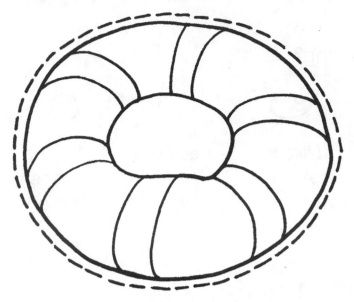

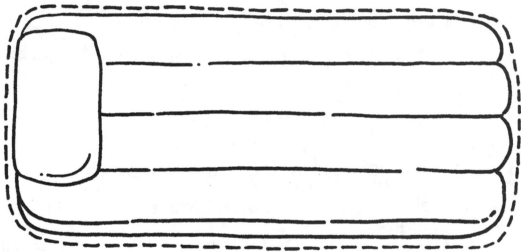

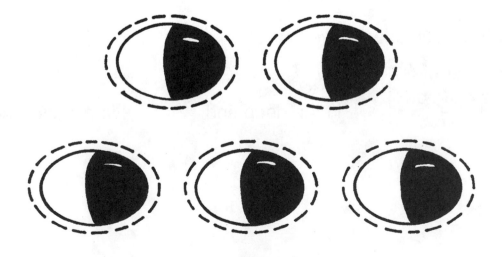

What Time Is It?

Math Skills

- reading/writing time
- numbers 1–12
- one-to-one correspondence

Materials

- reproducible glyph patterns and legend from pages 65–67
- completed alarm clock glyph
- scissors
- glue or paste
- crayons
- paper fasteners
- index cards
- paper plates

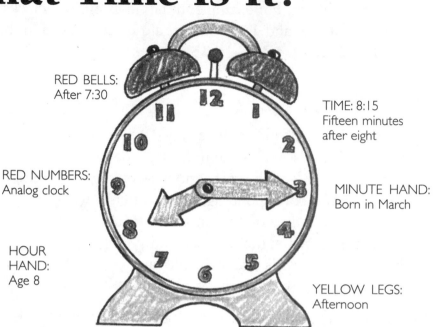

RED BELLS:
After 7:30

TIME: 8:15
Fifteen minutes after eight

RED NUMBERS:
Analog clock

MINUTE HAND:
Born in March

HOUR HAND:
Age 8

YELLOW LEGS:
Afternoon

Creating the Glyph

Distribute copies of the alarm clock glyph patterns and the legend to students. Review the legend, one characteristic at a time, as you display a glyph you have completed. Then distribute the other materials, and invite students to use the legend to create their own personal alarm clock glyph. (Note: Point out to students the difference between *analog* and *digital* clocks.)

1. Students can paste the clock face onto a paper plate to make a sturdier clock. They can fasten the hands with a paper fastener so that they will move.

2. Provide index cards for students to record the time according to Step 6 on the legend. For example, if a student's clock shows the hour hand pointing to 8 and the minute hand pointing to 3, that student would write the time *8:15* and *fifteen minutes after eight.*

Critical Thinking

Have students work in small groups to do this activity. Ask them to place their alarm clock glyphs so that the whole group can see the times on the clocks. Have them put their clocks in order according to the times shown. For example, if the times on four clocks were 4:15, 2:30, 6:25, and 1:30, they would be sequenced in this order: **1:30   2:30   4:15   6:25**

Explore More

☀ **Math** Have students play a three-way time matching game. Use a classroom display clock. Prepare index cards with times written as on a digital clock and corresponding times written in words. Show a time on the classroom clock. Ask students to match the time shown by finding the index cards that show the same time on a digital clock and in words.

☀ **Language Arts** As a class, create a list of all the things students do in a typical school day. Together, sequence the events of the school day in their proper order. Invite students to create stories of their school day, mentioning the events the class has sequenced.

☀ **Math** Have students estimate how many times they can say the alphabet or write the numbers from one to ten in a minute. Write their estimates on the chalkboard. Then invite them to do the task, and record the actual time it took. Try this with several tasks; see if students' estimates improve, and discuss whether they over- or underestimate the amount of time the tasks will take.

Another time estimation activity is to have students close their eyes and raise their hands when they think a minute has gone by. Try this several times and see if students' estimates improve.

☀ **Math** Create a list of things students might do during a day, such as the following:

Arrive at school	Go to bed
Go to soccer practice	Eat dinner

Discuss when it is important to know the exact time and when it is not so important. Ask students to sort the activities accordingly.

The Grouchy Ladybug by Eric Carle. HarperCollins Publishers, New York, 1977.

A grouchy ladybug wants to pick a fight with an assortment of animals. Each hour she stops and finds a different animal to taunt. As each hour passes, the animals get bigger and bigger. Each page includes an illustration of a clock.

Pigs on a Blanket by Amy Axelrod. Simon & Schuster Books, 1996.

As the Pig Family prepares for a trip to the beach, they discover that everything takes some time. They arrive at the beach just in time to eat and jump in the water before they realize that the beach is closing.

(1) How would you rather tell time?

Numbers on Clock	**red**	**blue**
	with an analog clock	with a digital clock

(2) How old are you? Point the hour hand to the number that tells your age.

(3) In what month were you born? Point the minute hand to the month.

Minute Hand	1 January	5 May	9 September
	2 February	6 June	10 October
	3 March	7 July	11 November
	4 April	8 August	12 December

(4) What is your favorite time of the day?

Color of Legs	**green**	**yellow**	**red**
	morning	afternoon	evening

(5) When do you wake up on school days?

Color of Bells	**green**	**yellow**	**red**
	before 6:30	between 6:30 and 7:30	after 7:30

(6) What time does your clock show? Write the time two different ways.

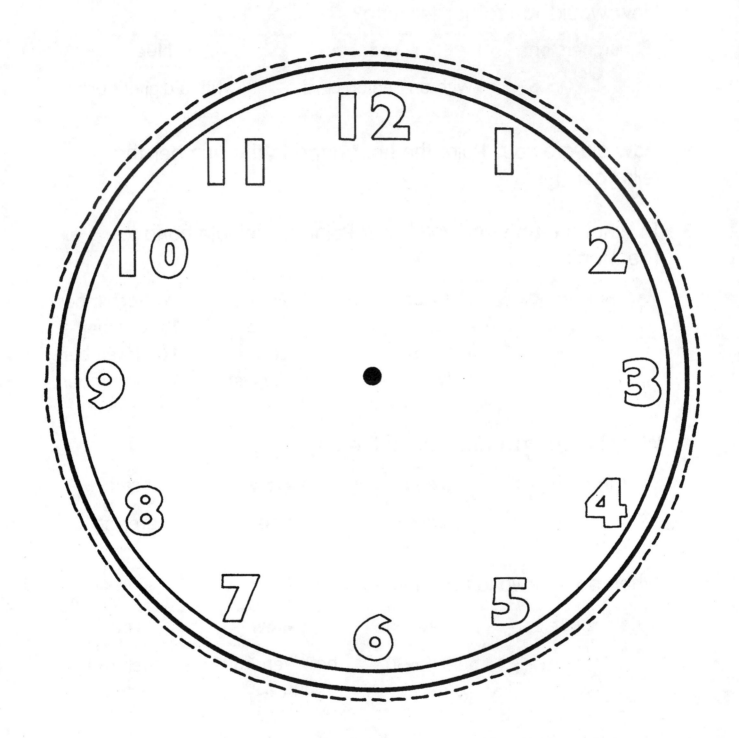

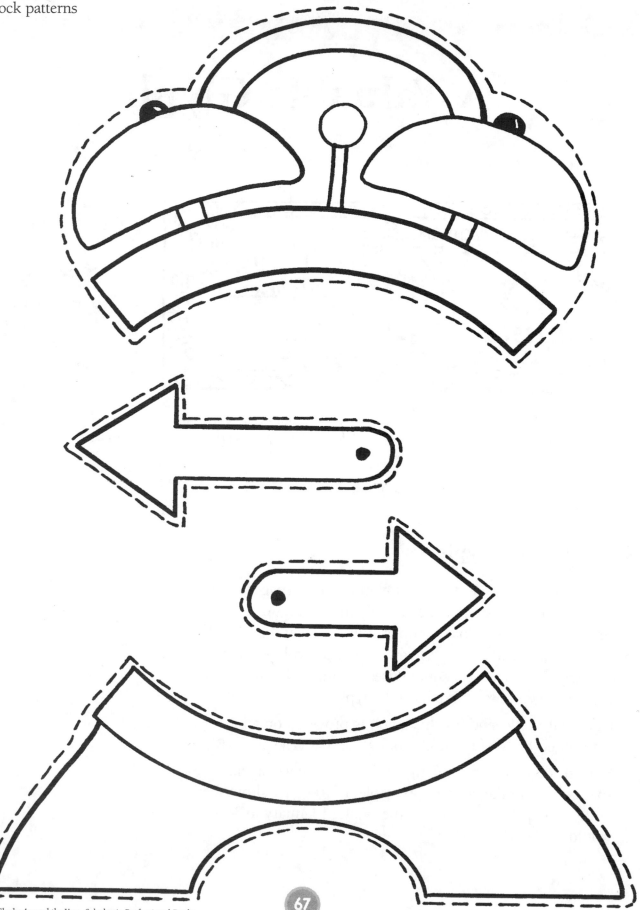

A Valuable Glyph

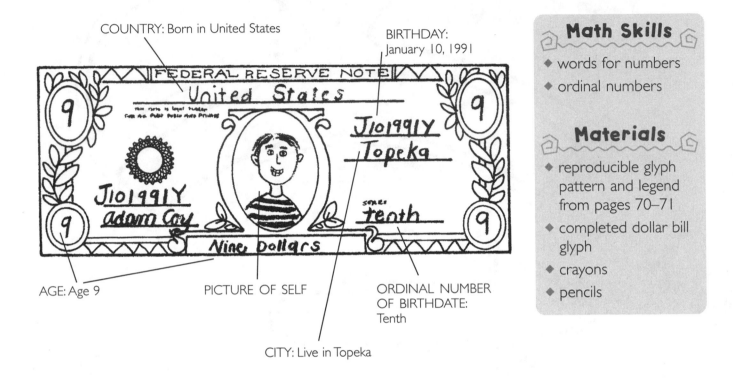

COUNTRY: Born in United States

BIRTHDAY: January 10, 1991

AGE: Age 9

PICTURE OF SELF

ORDINAL NUMBER OF BIRTHDATE: Tenth

CITY: Live in Topeka

Math Skills

- words for numbers
- ordinal numbers

Materials

- reproducible glyph pattern and legend from pages 70–71
- completed dollar bill glyph
- crayons
- pencils

Creating the Glyph

Distribute copies of the dollar bill glyph pattern (page71) to students. (You might reproduce the glyph pattern on green paper to imitate the color of a dollar bill.) Review the legend, one characteristic at a time, as you display a glyph you have completed. Then ask students to use crayons and pencils to create their own personal dollar bill glyph.

1. Note that the legend for this glyph is provided on an anno-tated copy of the dollar bill glyph pattern (page 70).

2. Help students identify the information that goes on each space of the dollar bill. For example, for the "serial number" of the bill, a student born on the tenth of January in 1991 would write J1011991Y.

Critical Thinking

Ask students to examine the number/letter sequence that appears on the left above the signature on their bill.

1. Use ordinal numbers to refer to the dates, and have students organize themselves from first to thirtieth according to the day of the month on which they were born.

2. Ask students to group themselves by birth month. For this they should check the letters that appear at the beginning and end of the month in which they were born.

3. Help each group organize themselves in order of date of birth within the month.

Explore More

☼ **Math** Ask students to determine the total "value" of the glyphs they made, based on the numbers represented on the dollar bills they have created. For example, if there are ten students in your class who are eight years old and eight students who are nine years old, the total value of the glyphs would be one-hundred fifty-two dollars. Depending on the math skills of your class, have students add or multiply to find the total value, or use a calculator to find this figure.

☼ **Social Studies** Invite students to bring in currency from other countries, either coins or paper money. Have some examples on hand from the United States as well. Use magnifying glasses to examine the money, and ask students to discuss or write about their findings.

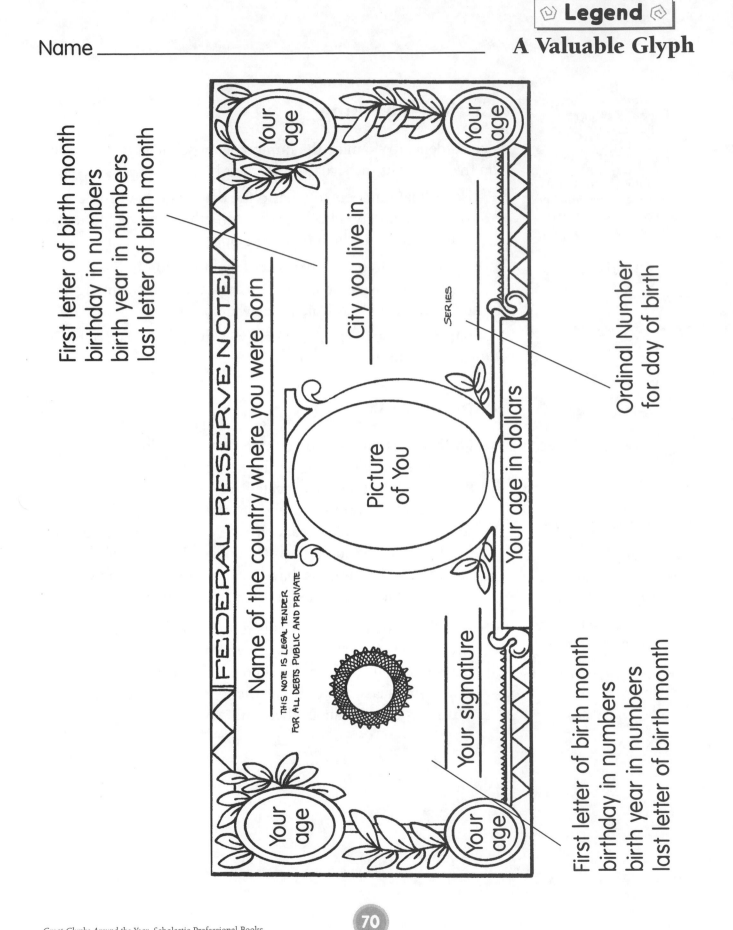

First letter of birth month
birthday in numbers
birth year in numbers
last letter of birth month

Your age

Your age

City you live in

SERIES

Ordinal Number
for day of birth

FEDERAL RESERVE NOTE

Name of the country where you were born

THIS NOTE IS LEGAL TENDER
FOR ALL DEBTS PUBLIC AND PRIVATE

Picture
of You

Your signature

Your age in dollars

Your age

Your age

First letter of birth month
birthday in numbers
birth year in numbers
last letter of birth month

FEDERAL RESERVE NOTE

THIS NOTE IS LEGAL TENDER
FOR ALL DEBTS PUBLIC AND PRIVATE

SERIES

Brush Up on Glyphs!

WHITE TOOTHPASTE:
Have gone to the dentist

BRISTLES:
Use electric toothbrush

BLUE STRIPE:
Put tooth under pillow

GREEN HANDLE:
Lost 4 or more teeth

THREE STARS ON BRUSH:
Brush three times daily

Math Skills

- measurement: time
- one-to-one correspondence
- counting

Materials

- reproducible glyph patterns and legend from pages 74–75
- completed toothbrush glyph
- scissors
- construction paper
- glue or paste
- crayons

Creating the Glyph

Distribute copies of the toothbrush patterns and the legend to students. Review the legend, one characteristic at a time, as you display a glyph you have completed. Then distribute the other materials, and invite students to use the legend to create their own personal toothbrush glyph.

1. Have students paste all the elements of the glyph onto construction paper for a sturdy backing.

2. Ask students to paste the toothpaste above the bristles of the brush so the shape and color of the bristles remain visible.

Critical Thinking

Create toothbrush logic problems. For example:

☼ I brush my teeth twice a day. When a tooth falls out, I put it under my pillow. I use a regular toothbrush.
Which toothbrush is mine?

Literature LINKS

The Bear's Toothache
by David McPhail. Little, Brown and Company, 1988.
A little boy meets a big bear who has a bad toothache. He tries to think of ways to help the bear remove the tooth.

The Tiger Has a Toothache by Mary Morgan. National Geographic Society, 1999.
At a popular zoo a tiger gets a toothache, and veterinarians use scientific knowledge and a caring attitude to cure him.

☼ I have lost two teeth this year. I use an electric toothbrush. I have not gone to the dentist this year. Which toothbrush is mine?

Give additional clues as needed, and have students guess the answers. Once you have modeled the creation of some logic problems, invite volunteers to give similar clues to their classmates.

Explore More

☼ **Science, Health** Invite a dentist or the school nurse to visit the classroom. Prior to the visit, have students brainstorm a list of questions to ask. Ask the dentist or nurse to talk about how to maintain good dental health and to demonstrate good brushing techniques.

☼ **Math** Have students keep track of the amount of time (in minutes) they spend each week brushing their teeth. Record this information on a graph. Set a goal of how much time per week each child should be brushing, based on the information you receive from the dentist. Determine whether your class is brushing enough or if you are short of the goal and by how many minutes. As an extra challenge, you may want students to figure out how much time they spend brushing their teeth in a week, a month, or even a year.

☼ **Math, Language Arts** Keep an ongoing tooth tally of the number of teeth lost each month by students in your class. Invite students to create imaginary stories about what they do with teeth that fall out and what might happen to all these teeth.

☼ **Math, Science** List several brands of popular toothpaste. Have students create a graph showing how many prefer each brand. Ask students to bring in packages from a variety of brands, and have them determine the ingredients of popular toothpastes. By making charts, lists, or tables, students can

Name _____

1 How many teeth have you lost this year?

Color of Handle	red	blue	green
	0 or 1 teeth	2 or 3 teeth	4 or more teeth

2 How many times do you brush your teeth each day?

Stars on Handle	1	2	3
	once	twice	three times

3 What kind of toothbrush do you use?

Bristles		
	electric	regular

4 What do you do when you lose a tooth?

Color of Stripe	blue	green	red	yellow
	I put it under my pillow.	I put it in a special box.	I throw it away.	None of my teeth have fallen out.

5 Have you gone to the dentist this year?

Color of Toothpaste	white	blue
	yes	no

Toothbrush pattern

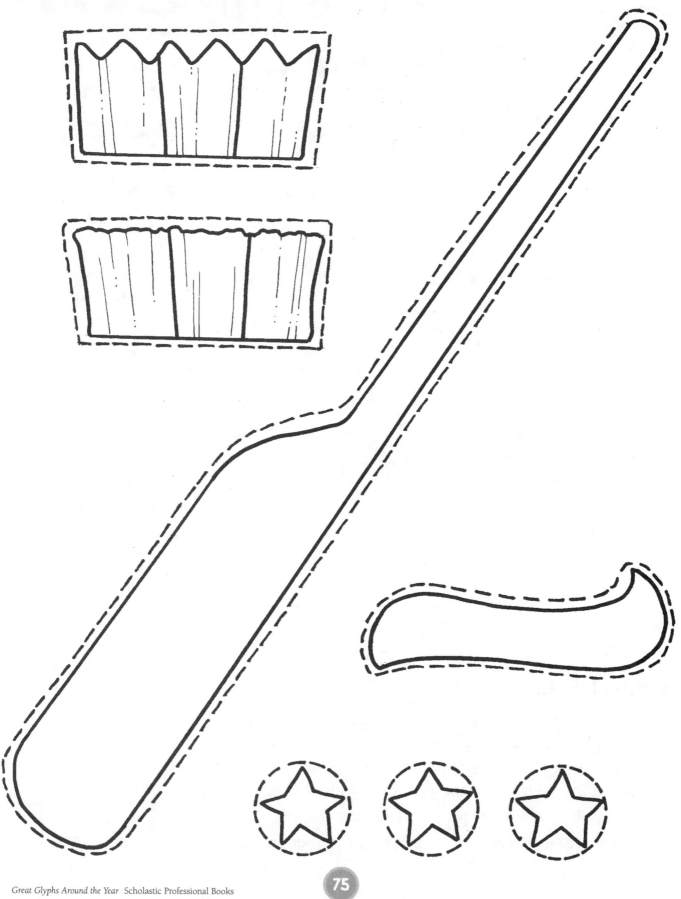

Roll 'Em!

YELLOW HELMET:
Like to visit relatives

LARGE MOUTH:
Water

LEFT ARM UP, RIGHT
ARM DOWN: Birthday
in another month

BLUE PADS:
Like ice cream

RED SKATES: Swim

Math Skills

- directionality: up,
  down; left, right
- months of the year
- size: small, medium,
  large

Materials

- reproducible glyph
  patterns and legend
  from pages 78–80
- completed in-line
  skater glyph
- construction paper
- glue or paste
- scissors
- crayons

Creating the Glyph

Distribute copies of the glyph patterns and the legend to students. Review the legend, one characteristic at a time, as you display a skater glyph you have completed. Then distribute the other materials, and invite students to create their own personal skater glyph.

Critical Thinking

The first four items on the legend specify preferences. Talk with students about these preferences, or opinions, and how they differ from item 5, which are reports of facts. Ask students to develop additional items for the legend that will reveal:

1. Facts, such as number of pairs of skates in family;

2. Opinions, or preferences, such as favorite television sport.

Explore More

☼ **Math, Language Arts** Have students list all the other sports they can think of that use wheels. Then suggest other categories for sports-related classifications. Have students make lists for such things as:

◆ Sports that you play alone

◆ Team sports

◆ Sports that use a ball

☼ **Science** Obtain some wheels of various sizes: for example, a tire, a bicycle wheel, a child's wagon wheel. Have students predict how far each one will roll and which will go the farthest. In an unobstructed area, ask students to roll each wheel until it stops, measure the distance, and check their predictions. Have students determine whether or not the radius of the wheel has any correlation to the distance the wheel rolls.

☼ **Safety, Language Arts** Talk with students about safe practices for in-line skating. As a class, write a list of safety rules. Encourage students to think of rules that will enhance their own safety as skaters, such as wearing protective clothing and helmets. Have students write a persuasive letter to a friend trying to convince him or her to wear this protective gear.

1 Which summer activity would you rather do?

Color of In-line Skates	red	yellow	blue	green
	swim	ride my bike	go to camp	skate

2 What do you like to drink?

Size of Mouth	small	medium	large
	lemonade or juice	soda	water

3 Where would you like to go on vacation?

Color of Helmet	blue	red	yellow
	the beach	the mountains	to visit relatives

4 What is your favorite summer dessert?

Color of Pads	blue	red	yellow	green
	ice cream	watermelon	popsicles	something else

5 When do you celebrate your birthday?

Arms	both arms up	both arms down	right arm up, left arm down	left arm up, right arm down
	in June	in July	in August	in another month

Great Glyphs Around the Year Scholastic Professional Books

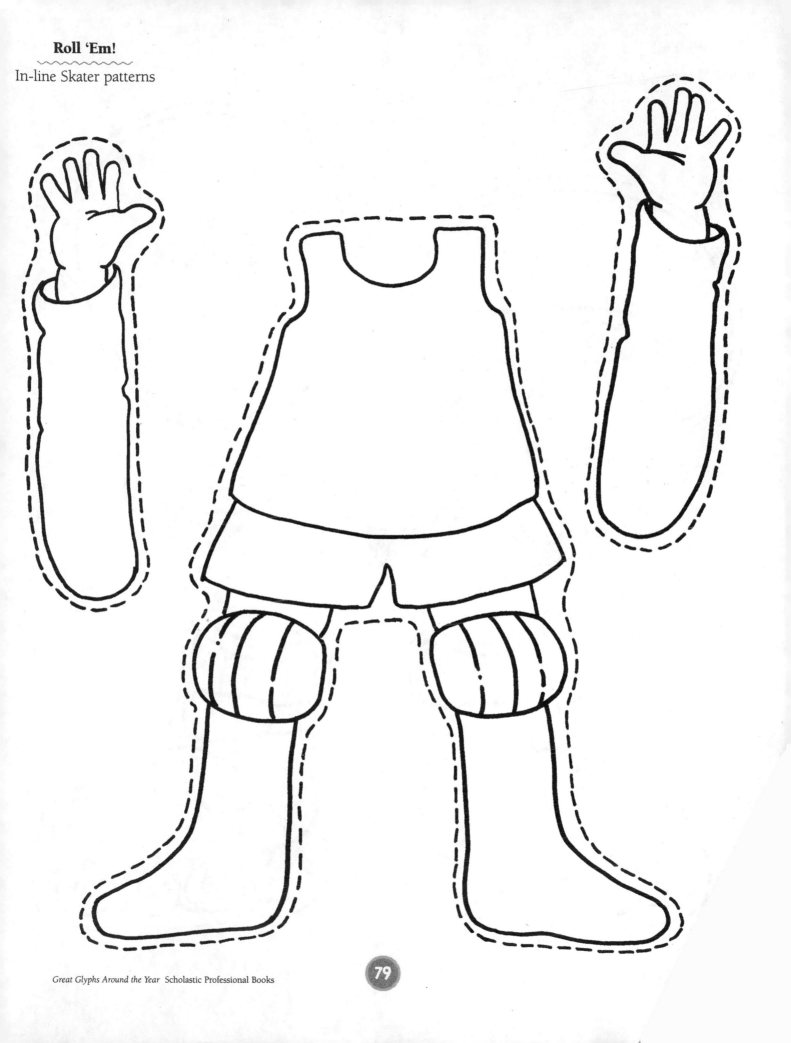

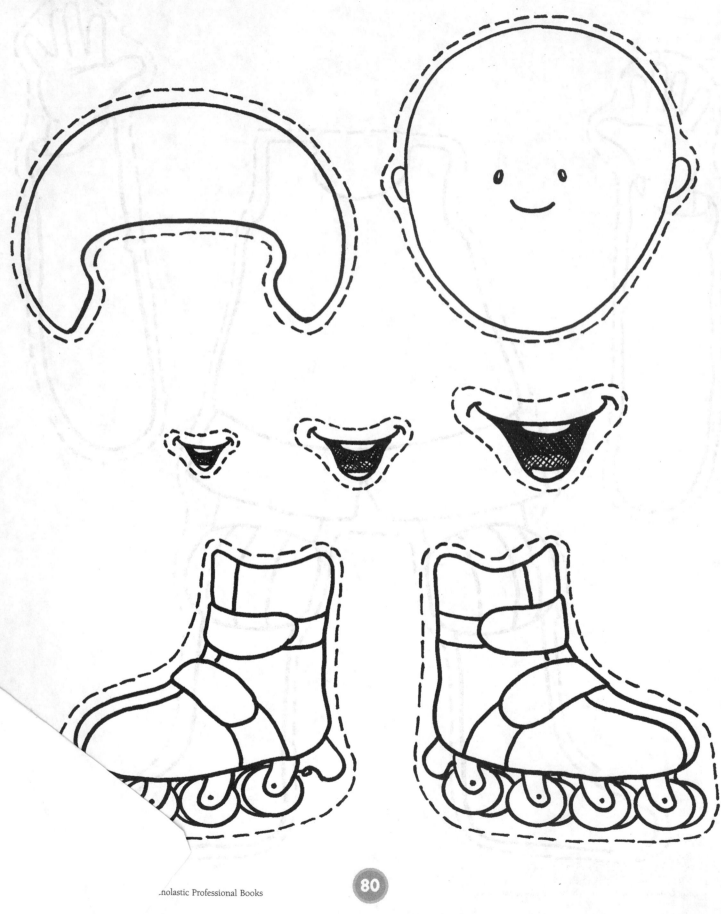

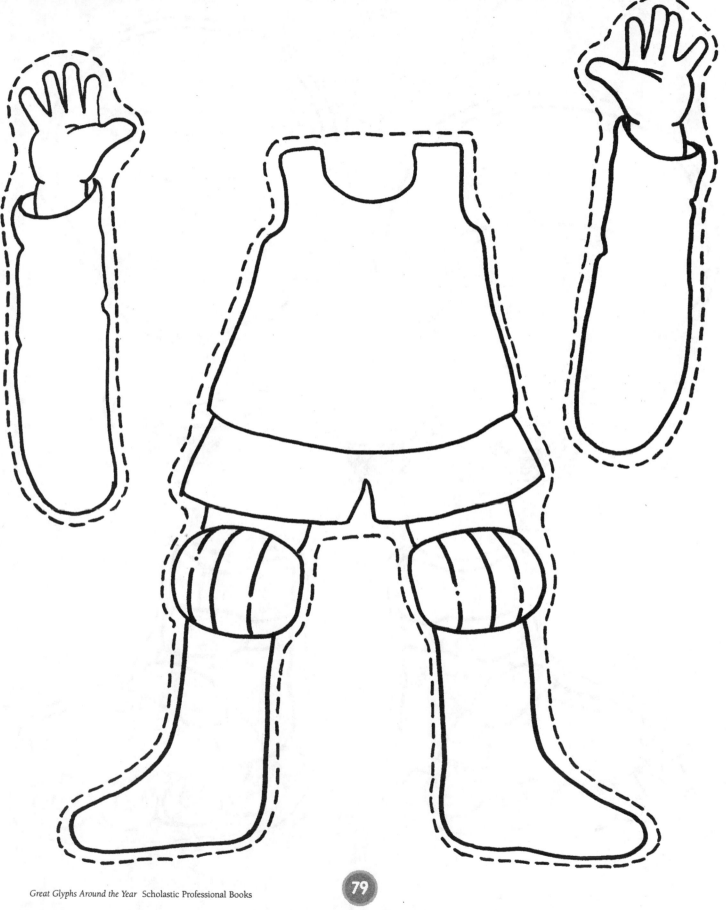

Great Glyphs Around the Year Scholastic Professional Books

Great Glyphs Around the Year Scholastic Professional Books